The Foundation Administrator

The
Foundation
Administrator

A Study of Those Who Manage America's Foundations

Arnold J. Zurcher

and

Jane Dustan

RUSSELL SAGE FOUNDATION
NEW YORK

PUBLICATIONS OF RUSSELL SAGE FOUNDATION

Russell Sage Foundation was established in 1907 by Mrs. Russell Sage for the improvement of social and living conditions in the United States. In carrying out its purpose the Foundation conducts research under the direction of members of the staff or in close collaboration with other institutions, and supports programs designed to develop and demonstrate productive working relations between social scientists and other professional groups. As an integral part of its operations, the Foundation from time to time publishes books or pamphlets resulting from these activities. Publication under the imprint of the Foundation does not necessarily imply agreement by the Foundation, its Trustees, or its staff with the interpretations or conclusions of the authors.

Russell Sage Foundation
230 Park Avenue, New York, N.Y. 10017

Contents

Introduction   1

What is a Foundation?, 1
Definition of the Administrator, 4
Foundation Typology, 4
Responses to Study's Foundation Questionnaire—The Study's
    Universe of Foundations, 6
The Administrator Career Questionnaire, 16
The Study's Data File, 18

1. The Extent of Foundation Staffing—Absence of Staffing Policies   19

Traditional Constraints on Staffing, 26
Absence of Staffing Policies, 32
Influence of the Tax Reform Act of 1969, 35

2. The Employment and Specialization of Staff   37

Job Descriptions of Foundation Staff, 38
Staff-Trustee Relationship in Program Matters, 44
Job Mobility in the Staffed Foundations, 47
In-Service Orientation and Training Programs, 48
The Use of Consultants, 50

3. Preparation, Recruitment, and Retirement of Staff   55

Educational Backgrounds, 55
Previous Professional Experience, 56
Opinions on Training for Foundation Service, 60
Some Evidence of an Opposing Trend, 65
Recruiting Foundation Staff, 66

List of Tables

Introduction

Chapter 1

Chapter 2

Chapter 3

Chapter 4

Chapter 5

Chapter 6

Appendix I

List of Figures

Preface

This volume is a report of a study conducted throughout 1970 and into 1971 of the people who manage American foundations and determine their policies. Although the principal concern has been those individuals who derive their livelihood and professional satisfactions from serving foundations, attention has also been directed to that generous percentage of foundations that have no paid executives and accordingly rely on the donor, trustees, and others for the discharge of ordinary administrative responsibilities. In focusing on the paid managers or administrators, their selection and training, their professional satisfactions, and their opinions of foundation employment, the study has necessarily involved the asset size of foundations, their founding auspices, their location, their programming, and other considerations relating to their management. But since this is a study of staffing or personnel policies, matters related to the broader aspects of management have been considered only incidentally. Management policies are, to be sure, inextricably involved in staffing policies, but because the study's focus was the latter, its directors have alluded to management policies and practices only as they are relevant or essential to an understanding of this narrower aim.

Only if the people who know the field of a study are generous in extending counsel and information is the study assured of the hard data and informed opinion that authenticate its tabulations and conclusions. This aid was extended generously by hundreds of foundation staff people, and we, the authors, are immensely grateful for it. These volunteers were willing to suffer the infliction of the questionnaires that appear in Appendix III and to complete them conscientiously, often at considerable expense of time and energy. It is impossible to thank each individual personally for his or her contribution. Hence, we are relying on this more general acknowledgement of their assistance. We express the hope that each of them may find vicarious satisfaction of authorship—albeit none of the responsibility or liability —in the knowledge that his contribution is embedded in paragraph after paragraph, and table after table in this volume.

In expressing our gratitude to those who gave assistance, we wish to single out a number of people for special mention. First, we wish to acknowledge our indebtedness to Orville G. Brim, Jr., president of Russell Sage Foundation, and to Manning M. Pattillo, former president of The Foundation Center. In addition to designing the study and developing its original working outline, these men provided valuable counsel and encouragement throughout the study's every stage, including the manuscript stage. Their colleagues on the staffs of Russell Sage Foundation and The Foundation Center also provided indispensable assistance. At the Center, the authors are particularly indebted to Marianna O. Lewis, editor of *The Foundation Directory,* Edna Brigham, at the time, secretary of the Center, and Harvey B. Matthews, Jr., Center vice president and editor of *Foundation News.* None of these people failed to respond generously when we needed their expert assistance. Mrs. Lewis was especially helpful as a constant source of up-to-date and detailed information on new foundations and their personnel or on existing foundations that had expanded or were contemplating expansion of their staff.

As for members of the staff of Russell Sage Foundation where the project had its physical "home," they gave the word "home" its true meaning by the warmth of their hospitality and their constant effort to assist us in overcoming the physical and intellectual hurdles we encountered. Hugh F. Cline of the Foundation staff spent countless hours with the study's staff, including the authors of this report, introducing us to and guiding us through the intricacies of computer usage. He thereby enabled the project to use a technological tool that expanded the value of the data and enabled it to approach the status of a contemporary quantitative study. Valuable counsel and other forms of assistance were rendered by the following Russell Sage Foundation staff: Wilbert E. Moore, currently professor of law at the University of Denver, Donald R. Young, president emeritus of the Foundation and honorary trustee, and Jean C. Yoder, editor.

Among a host of others who were especially generous of their time and assistance, we wish to mention F. Emerson Andrews, president emeritus of The Foundation Center and Thomas R. Buckman, president of the Center, each of whom read the manuscript of this report; David Freeman, president of the Council on Foundations, who was particularly helpful in our efforts to enlist the cooperation of the community foundations; Henry Sellin, executive director of the New York University Institute on Charitable Foundations; Ronald B. Szczypkowski associated at the time with the Milbank Memorial Fund; W. McNeil Lowry, vice president of the Ford Foundation; William P. Gormbley of the Ford Foundation; and Marvin Bower, director of McKinsey & Company.

We also wish to express appreciation of the aid constantly tendered by members of the project's own staff. Our special thanks go to Rita Barusich, secretary and research assistant, who worked with us for more than a year and played a major role in preparing the data for the computer and in developing the tables and charts based on those data. Four other staff members associated with the project for shorter periods—Ellen Stuttle, Steven Rosenthal, Beulah Gleich, and Peter Yastishak—also made important contributions to the completion of this undertaking.

Finally, we wish to express our gratitude to the members of the panel of foundation experts and executives who served as the Advisory Committee for the study. The twelve members of this committee, some of whom have been mentioned earlier, are: Derek C. Bok, president, Harvard University; Marvin Bower, director, McKinsey & Company; George M. Buckingham, recently retired executive director of the Esso Education Foundation; Charles S. Hamilton, Jr., formerly president of the Andrew W. Mellon Foundation; J. George Harrar, president of the Rockefeller Foundation; W. McNeil Lowry, vice president of the Ford Foundation; John R. May, executive director and secretary of the San Francisco Foundation; Robert K. Merton, professor of sociology at Columbia University; Lloyd N. Morrisett, president of the John and Mary R. Markle Foundation; Frederick D. Patterson, formerly president of the Phelps-Stokes Fund and now president of the Robert R. Moton Memorial Foundation, Inc.; David B. Truman, president of Mount Holyoke College; and Martha R. Wallace, vice president and executive director of the Henry Luce Foundation, Inc. Both in their collective capacity as a committee and as individuals, these distinguished persons assisted in securing access to data, counselled on the direction of the study, and read and advised on the manuscript of this report prior to its delivery to the publisher. Several of the members were particularly generous of time spent on the manuscript. The reviews they submitted saved us from errors of fact and interpretation and improved both the structure and style of the manuscript.

Because various institutions and a great many individuals have been so generous in lending assistance to this project, it is especially necessary that, in acknowledging that assistance, it be made abundantly clear that none of them—either individual or institution—bears any responsibility for the form or content of this report. The directors of the study and authors of this report are solely responsible for whatever data have been included or excluded, for editorial judgment, and for all decisions affecting the report's content, style, and tone. The authors wish to make it particularly clear that no responsibility for the conduct of the study or its results attaches to The Foundation Center or Russell Sage Foundation, to anyone connected with those organizations, or to the Advisory Committee or to any of the twelve members of that Committee. Let it be reiterated that the study's directors and the authors of this report are alone responsible for whatever shortcomings the study may have and for whatever information and opinions this report conveys to the reader.

ARNOLD J. ZURCHER
JANE DUSTAN

New York City
February 1972

Introduction

Although foundations have played a prominent and, on the whole, commendable role in promoting American scientific and cultural life, the way in which they operate and make decisions remains largely a mystery to the general public. Often, it is a mystery to that part of the public which is otherwise well informed. This study of the foundation administrator has been undertaken in the belief that systematic knowledge about the managers of an enterprise is a key to understanding the enterprise itself. Knowledge based chiefly on empirical data that have been objectively analyzed and interpreted is especially useful. In any case, a better understanding of those who administer foundations will, it is believed, make foundations themselves more understandable and more meaningful, and thus help to clear away much of whatever mystery or ignorance may currently surround those institutions.

What Is a Foundation?

Before proceeding with a study of the foundation administrator, it is necessary to identify the organization that employs him. This is a difficult task, for a foundation does not lend itself to precise definition. The difficulty is aggravated by the diversity of activities of organizations that call themselves foundations. Some may be essentially research organizations or academic institutions. Others may be social welfare agencies or even trade associations. The word "foundation" also graces the names of fund-raising organizations, community welfare funds, patriotic societies, church endowments, college and alumni funds, and voluntary health organizations.

The diversity of foundations' legal structures also contributes impre-

1

cision to the concept of the organization. Some foundations are corporate entities, others are trusts, and a few are mere associations. A corporate foundation[1] is established under a charter granted by some governmental authority. Because of its origin, a corporate foundation somewhat resembles the legal concept of a business corporation. Unlike the latter, however, a corporate foundation is operated not for private profit or gain but for the benefit of the general public, and those who direct and administer it may not derive a private benefit from it.[2] A trust, on the other hand, is created by an individual who, by means of an appropriate legal instrument, transfers title to property to a group of individuals (or possibly to an institution such as a bank) called trustees, who thereafter hold the property and (usually) administer it for the benefit of others. In the case of a trust established as a foundation, the beneficiaries are the public or named public entities. Often, a trust is so restricted as to its administration and purpose that it has little in common with the usually more liberal corporate concept of a foundation. Table 1, adapted from *The Foundation Directory, Edition 3*,[3] classifies foundations as to their legal form. It shows that about two-thirds of all foundations are corporations and that about one-third are trusts.

Table 1. The Legal Form of Foundations and the Number Created During Each of Several Decades of the Twentieth Century

Period	Corporations	Trusts	Other	Total
Before 1900	19 (73%)	6 (23%)	1 (4%)	26
1900–1909	12 (67%)	6 (33%)	0 ——	18
1910–1919	39 (51%)	36 (48%)	1 (1%)	76
1920–1929	125 (71%)	52 (29%)	0 ——	177
1930–1939	194 (66%)	98 (33%)	2 (1%)	294
1940–1949	1,116 (71%)	450 (28%)	17 (1%)	1,583
1950–1959	2,524 (66%)	1,253 (33%)	40 (1%)	3,817
1960——*	497 (66%)	227 (30%)	30 (4%)	754
Total	4,526 (67%)	2,128 (32%)	91 (1%)	6,745

* The records for the period since 1960 are fragmentary.

---

[1] As used here, the phrase "corporate foundation" refers solely to the *legal form* of a foundation. It does not identify foundations founded by business interests or business corporations. In this volume such foundations are termed "company-sponsored foundations."

[2] Cases of abuse of the purposes of foundations, revealed by some recent investigations, hardly affect the validity of this statement.

[3] "Legal Form of 6,654 Foundations, by Decade of Origin after 1900," *The Foundation Directory, Edition 3*, New York: Russell Sage Foundation, p. 13.

A third factor contributing to the difficulty of clarifying the concept of the foundation results from the way in which the federal government has handled the foundation's tax-exempt status. Over the years, the government has commingled foundations with other tax-exempt organizations such as churches, private schools and colleges, universities, museums, and the like, and extended to foundations essentially the same treatment it gives these other organizations. Indeed, it is only since the tax reform legislation of 1969, which levied a tax on foundations, that the government has begun to distinguish between the tax-exempt status of the foundation and that of other nonprofit organizations and to arrive at a distinct, if still not too clearly articulated, definition of a private foundation.

For the purposes of this study, a private foundation is defined as an entity established under private auspices and privately governed, an entity that has its own endowment and that uses the income, or the endowment itself, in support of various educational, religious, cultural, or other public charitable objectives. More succinctly, a private foundation may be defined as a private philanthropic agency that uses its funds to promote the public welfare. According to The Foundation Center, there were in the United States as of 1970 at least 24,000 foundations that fulfilled the requirements of this definition.[4] Many of these are small and their philanthropic role is relatively insignificant.[5] Occasionally, in the following pages, reference will be made to this figure of 24,000 foundations. Normally, however, the

---

[4] The estimate of the entire foundation universe is based on records and extrapolations of the Center, which obtains its data on the number, size, and activity of foundations from various sources. These include returns filed annually with the United States Treasury (Form 990–A, now 990) by virtually all tax-exempt organizations, including all foundations (which are now also required to file Form 990–AR); from published and unpublished reports, questionnaires, and other information sent to the Center by foundations; from requests for information on organizational matters made of the Center by new foundations; from a study of the supplements to the list of exempt organizations issued from time to time by the Treasury; and from news clippings and miscellaneous sources. From these data the Center has, since 1964, maintained a cumulative tally of existing and new foundations in each of the fifty states, a tally that by 1970 had reached a national figure in excess of 36,000. If allowance is made for those organizations that do not fit the definition of a foundation and for organizations that have lost their exemption, been dissolved, or become inactive, Center authorities believe that a conservative estimate for all foundations in the United States in 1970 should not be less than 24,000.

[5] In preparing *Edition 3* of *The Foundation Directory*, The Foundation Center tabulated only those of the estimated 24,000 private foundations that had assets of at least $200,000 and/or distributed annually at least $10,000 in grants. The resulting number was 6,803 foundations. See *Directory*, p. 5.

study will refer to its own universe of foundations, to be described in greater detail subsequently.

Definition of the Administrator

In identifying those individuals with whom this study is concerned, that is, foundation administrators, the word "administrator" has been used to comprehend all persons concerned with any aspect of the management of a foundation. In its broadest sense, therefore, the word embraces all those who derive their livelihood and occupational satisfactions from serving a foundation in a post above the clerical level. Included are not only a foundation's chief executive officer, but also those who serve in a staff capacity, either in the internal administration of the foundation or as program executives or field representatives. On a subsequent page, an attempt is made to give somewhat greater precision to the concept of the foundation administrator by providing eleven basic categories of foundation positions. The categories range from chief executive to staff specialist.[6] Part-time administrators, provided they are paid and not considered temporary, are included in the census of administrators. Consultants, on the other hand, are not so included.

In the following chapters, the administrator, as thus defined and classified, will be studied in some detail. Consideration will be given to his formal training and preparation for foundation service, the conditions that affect his recruitment for such service, his role as principal officer or member of a staff, the nature of his rewards, economic and psychic, and his own attitude toward his job and toward the place of foundations in our society. Other chapters, especially Chapters 1, 2, and 7, explore some of the ideological values, managerial considerations, and social forces that inhibit or foster the employment of paid administrators by foundations.

Foundation Typology

Foundations vary considerably. Hence, for subsequent discussion and analysis, it is not meaningful to combine all foundations. Instead, a system must be devised for classifying foundations into more homogeneous subgroups so that analysis may be conducted within these subgroups. A theoretical framework for such classification into subgroups, available in other areas of social science research, is not available in the case of foundations. The study's typology must therefore be based on the authors' assessment

---

[6] See Chapter 2.

of dimensions meaningful to the world of foundations and meaningful for analysis. These dimensions are as follows:

——Asset size
——Program
——Founding auspices
——Founding auspices combined with program
——Staff size

Other possible dimensions that occasionally prove useful for classification are the geographical location of foundations and their volume of annual grants and expenditures. It is these seven dimensions that provide the basic classifications or the typology of foundations.

The first, asset size, is probably the most familiar, since it is normally used in any public discussion of foundations. Variations in asset size are considerable. The smallest foundation may possess only a few thousand dollars in assets, and probably the majority of foundations fall into this asset category. Other foundations may have millions, a few even hundreds of millions. The largest of all, the Ford Foundation, has assets close to $3 billion.

The foundation's program—the broad purpose for which funds are used—is an almost equally familiar basis for classifying foundations. Most private foundations make grants to individuals or to other organizations that, like the foundation, are tax-exempt or engage in tax-exempt activities. For the most part, these foundations serve as a kind of conduit between the foundation's original source of funds—the private donor—and the recipient grantee. For want of a better term, the study has labeled these foundations "supportive foundations" and their programs "supportive programs."

Other foundations may combine a conduit or supportive program with considerable innovative effort in designing and initiating research and demonstration projects. A very few foundations virtually confine themselves to this type of program. Usually, the projects are confided to the administration of others, that is, to legal grantees, but the foundation often retains a rather close informal relationship with the administration of the projects and, in certain cases, especially when the projects are situated outside the United States, the foundation may itself take over most of the actual administrative responsibility. The program of such a foundation might be denominated "project-oriented" and the foundation itself might be called a "project-oriented foundation." The terms normally used are "general purpose program" and "general purpose foundation." Usage rather than the literal meaning of the phrase "general purpose" commends its employment.

A distinct minority of private foundations devote virtually all their income to an "internal" or "in-house" program. They may support internally conducted research; or they may have established and become the sole support of some cultural activity such as a museum or symphony orchestra or of a social welfare activity such as a health or recreational program in a community. These foundations are usually known as "operating foundations."

The third dimension on which the study's foundation typology is based is a foundation's founding auspices, also a familiar classification in the foundation world. Usually, the origin lies with a private donor or his family, the resulting organization being labeled a "family foundation." Or, the founding agency may be a business, bank, or other profit-making organization and the foundation is called a "company-sponsored foundation." Finally, a foundation set up by certain interests in the community to distribute locally the income of trusts, legacies, and gifts, is called a "community foundation."

For the purpose of the study, founding auspices and program have been combined as a classification primarily because foundations of family origin embrace those with all types of program whereas foundations founded by companies or communities are usually engaged only in supportive activities. Hence, the study uses the compound classifications of "family supportive," "family general purpose," and "family operating foundations."

Staff size is obviously a dimension especially relevant to the study. This dimension has been used frequently to set apart the non-staffed foundations, those with only one or two staff people, and the few foundations that are rather well staffed.

A foundation's geographical location is a variable of minor importance but of some use in classifying foundations. Figure I shows five regions into which the United States has been divided. These are Northeast, Southeast, North Central, South Central, and West. Because so much foundation wealth and activity are concentrated in New York City, it has been set up as a sub-classification within the Northeast region.

Still another dimension of minor value in establishing a useful foundation typology is the volume of a foundation's grants and expenditures. For various reasons, the annual volume of grants and expenditures often bears no direct relation to the magnitude of the wealth of a foundation; hence, the volume of expenditures may be a more useful index of the social value of the foundation than its wealth. Moreover, grant and expenditure volume can occasionally be helpful in measuring a foundation's administrative costs.

Responses to Study's Foundation Questionnaire— The Study's Universe of Foundations

To secure the necessary institutional data for the study, an appropriate questionnaire was devised. Since the principal concern is the foundation administrator, every effort was made to include among the foundations to which the questionnaire was sent those that might employ full-time or part-time executive-level staff. To assist in identifying these foundations the following steps were taken: (1) all available current published reports of foundations, regardless of asset size, were examined for personnel; (2) where published foundation reports were not available, copies of the legally required return filed with the Internal Revenue Service (Form 990), available at The Foundation Center, were examined for staff for all foundations above $5 million in assets; (3) knowledgeable individuals were consulted about foundations with assets under $5 million to determine if any might employ staff. The Foundation Center was of special assistance in this connection, often calling attention to foundations that had recently undergone considerable development, including the appointment of staff for the first time or an increase in the number of staff.

Relying on information collected in this manner an initial mailing of the questionnaire was made to some 484 foundations. These were foundations with assets of $5 million or more, the majority of which, as a result of the study's preliminary investigation, were thought to have some paid staff. A slightly more elaborate version of the questionnaire was also sent to twenty-seven foundations that the study's directors had ascertained were more extensively staffed than any others and were also among the largest and most active in the country. Another mailing was subsequently made to 174 foundations with assets of $5 million or more that were understood to have no paid staff and still later this mailing was supplemented by another of about a hundred questionnaires to foundations with assets between $1 and $5 million including a number with assets below $1 million. Only a few of these were suspected of having some paid staff.

Response rates among the queried foundations varied. In general, the larger, richer, staffed foundations, those with assets of $100 million or more, responded to the questionnaire, although a disappointingly large fraction—some with considerable staffs—failed to do so. Table 2 which follows identifies the response rate to the questionnaire by foundations of different asset sizes.

Table 2. Response Rate to Questionnaire by Foundations of Various Asset Sizes

Asset size	Response Rate (Percent)
$100 million or more	75
$26–$99.9 million	68
$11–$25.9 million	53
$1–$10.9 million	40
Under $1 million	50

Figure I. Five Regional Groupings

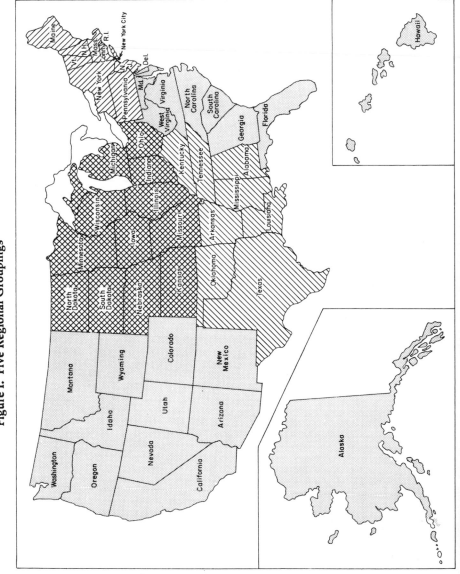

1. *Northeast*

Connecticut
Maine
Massachusetts
New Hampshire
New Jersey
New York (including New York City)
Pennsylvania
Rhode Island
Vermont

1a. *New York City*

2. *Southeast*

Delaware
District of Columbia
Florida
Georgia
Maryland
North Carolina
South Carolina
Virginia
West Virginia

3. *North Central*

Illinois
Indiana
Iowa
Kansas
Michigan
Minnesota
Missouri
Nebraska
North Dakota
Ohio
South Dakota
Wisconsin

4. *South Central*

Alabama
Arkansas
Kentucky
Louisiana
Mississippi
Oklahoma
Tennessee
Texas

5. *West*

Arizona
California
Colorado
Idaho
Montana
Nevada
New Mexico
Oregon
Utah
Washington
Wyoming

Alaska

Hawaii

Altogether some 785 questionnaires were distributed, and eventually the study received responses from 362 of the foundations that had received the questionnaire. To take care of cases in which a foundation known or suspected to have staff failed to respond, and of cases of unstaffed foundations of considerable wealth that the study's directors wished to include but that failed to complete the questionnaire, additional efforts were made to secure the necessary data. These included an examination of the reports of the foundation, if such reports existed, of information which the foundation may have filed with The Foundation Center, and of reports which the foundation had been required to file with the Internal Revenue Service. By these somewhat indirect means, data were secured on 300 foundations that, added to the 362 for which data were supplied by the questionnaire, provided the study with a universe of 662 foundations. The following tabulation summarizes the results of the questionnaire and the sources of the study's institutional data.

Table 3. Tabulation of Respondent and Non-Respondent Foundations to Questionnaire

Number of Foundations Receiving Questionnaire	Number of Foundations Responding to Questionnaire	Number of Non-respondent Foundations for which Data were Secured from Sources Other than Questionnaire	Number of Non-respondent Foundations on which no Data were Obtained
785	362 (46%)	300 (38%)	123 (16%)

With the exception of a further major source of information, to be described shortly, the dockets created for these 662 foundations—the study's universe of foundations—provided the original data analyzed in the study. This limited universe is admittedly only a segment of the totality of foundations. Nevertheless it is an important and a representative segment. Included are all the better known foundations, those whose names are likely to figure in the headlines or come to mind when the casually interested person thinks of a foundation. Moreover, this limited universe of 662 foundations embraces those in which the study is particularly interested, namely, foundations that employ personnel at the executive level. The directors of the study are confident that, as a result of their investigation, the study's universe embraces the employers of all full-time foundation executive personnel within an estimated margin of fifty people in addition to those definitely identified and enumerated.[7] It also includes all foundations with considerable assets that are administered without paid help and many of the foundations of moderate wealth that are unstaffed.

Also included are the foundations with part-time, permanently employed, paid staff although this category excludes board officers and trustees who devote a percentage of their time to foundation administration and who receive compensation for it. By definition, donors, or relatives of a donor, who devote time to the management of a foundation but receive no compensation, are also excluded. The only individuals not included in the census of paid foundation staff are employees of certain organizations, called foundations, which are really research organizations, and which, in most instances, formally requested that they be omitted from the study.

The composition of the limited study universe of foundations becomes clearer if some of the dimensions are applied to it that were used earlier in developing a foundation typology.

Thus, as respects asset size, Table 4 indicates that more than half of the foundations in this limited universe (373 foundations, 56.2 percent) have assets below $10 million, a fourth of them (166 foundations) have assets between $10 and $25 million, and about one-eighth (92 foundations, 13.9 percent) have assets between $25 and $100 million. All the wealthiest foundations ($100 million or more) are included except one which, late in 1971 following completion of the study, was said to have received a bequest of more than $1 billion, making it the second largest in the country.

As for founding auspices, another previously suggested basis for classifying the study's universe, it will be noted that in Table 5 that follows 80 percent (529 foundations) are family foundations. Company-sponsored and community foundations are decidedly less numerous, although their

Table 4. Asset Ranges of Foundations in Study Universe

Asset Range	Number of Foundations	Percentages
Under $1 million	54	8.2
1–9.9	319	48.0
10–24.9	166	25.1
25–99.9	92	13.9
100–299	21	3.2
300–1 billion	9	1.4
Over 1 billion	1	0.2
Total	662	100.0

[7] See Chapter 1.

Table 5. Classification of the Study's Universe of Foundations According to Founding Auspices

Auspices	Number of Foundations	Percent
Family	529	80
Company-sponsored	80	12
Community	50	7
Unclassified	3	1
Total	662	100

totals (eighty and fifty respectively) are a fair reflection of their number relative to that of the family foundations, which, as will be noted elsewhere, account for more than 90 percent of all foundations.

In outlining the study's foundation typology, founding auspices and program were combined to provide a classification. When that combined classification is applied in Table 6, by far the largest percentage of the study's universe is seen to fall into the family supportive category. Since, as noted earlier, company-sponsored and community foundations have largely supportive programs,[8] the total of primarily supportive foundations in the study's universe reaches almost 90 percent (588 foundations). Somewhat less than 5 percent (thirty foundations) are family foundations with a largely general purpose program, and somewhat over 6 percent (forty-one foundations) are classified as family operating foundations.

The combined classification of founding auspices and program of the study's universe of foundations is also cross-tabulated with asset size. The table suggests that the very limited number of family general purpose foundations are distributed among almost every asset category, although the majority are to be found in the wealthier brackets. Table 7 also indicates that the supportive type of program involves every asset category of foundation, with a concentration in the asset range of $1 to $25 million.

A further application of the study's typology to its universe of foundations concerns staffing. The resulting table identifies four categories. The first is 320 foundations, almost half of the study's universe (48.6 percent), that have no paid staff. They are operated by their trustees and are therefore identified as "trustee-operated." Occasionally, in subsequent tabulations, four or five of the foundations in this category are included in the second which has been denominated "trustee-operated with minor assistance." The difference is that although the 150 foundations in this category are also op-

---

[8] This being the case, the word "supportive" is omitted in later discussions of these two categories of foundations.

Table 6. Foundations in the Study's Universe Analyzed According to Founding Auspices and Program

Foundation Auspices/Program	Number of Foundations	Percentage
Family originated, largely supportive	458	69.5
Family originated, largely general purpose	30	4.6
Family originated, largely operating	41	6.2
Community, largely supportive	50	7.6
Company-sponsored, largely supportive	80	12.1
Total	659*	100.0

*It was not possible to classify three foundations.

Table 7. Auspices and Programs of Foundations of Various Asset Sizes

Asset Ranges of Foundations	Family General Purpose	Family Supportive	Family Operating	Community	Company Sponsored	Total
Under $1 million*	1	23	4	13	10	51
	3.3%	5.0%	9.8%	26.0%	12.5%	7.7%
$1–$9.99 million	5	227	24	19	44	319
	16.7%	49.6%	58.5%	38.0%	55.0%	48.4%
$10–$24.99 million	4	125	5	12	20	166
	13.3%	27.3%	12.2%	24.0%	25.0%	25.2%
$25–$99.99 million	10	65	7	5	5	92
	33.4%	14.2%	17.1%	10.0%	6.3%	14.0%
$100–$299.99 million	4	14	1	1	1	21
	13.3%	3.0%	2.4%	2.0%	1.2%	3.2%
$300 million	6	4	0	0	0	10
	20.0%	0.9%	0.0%	0.0%	0.0%	1.5%
Total	30	458	41	50	80	659**
	4.6%	69.5%	6.2%	7.6%	12.1%	100.0%

* To assist in reading this and subsequent tables, the following explanation is provided. The total number of foundations cross-tabulated is 659. The number 1, which appears in the first cell at the upper left of the table, indicates that there is one foundation with assets under $1 million and that this one foundation accounts for 3.3% of the foundations in the family general purpose category, of which there are 30 in the table. All other tables in this volume follow this scheme.
** It was not possible to classify three foundations.

Table 8. Staff Analysis of Foundations in the Study's Universe

Staff Range (or no staff)	Number of Foundations	Percent
Trustee-operated	320	48.6
Trustee-operated with minor assistance	150	22.8
1–3 full-time staff	150	22.8
More than 3 full-time staff	38	5.8
Total	658*	100.0

* Information was not available on four foundations.

erated by the trustees, there is generally a part-time or full-time functionary who assists them. Usually this person is of clerical stature—often a woman —who has been with the foundation for a good many years. In perhaps a fifth of these foundations, the person might be considered of junior executive stature who elsewhere in these pages will be counted as full-time executive staff. One hundred fifty foundations in the study's universe employ from one to three persons of executive stature full-time, and thirty-eight foundations—about 6 percent of the total—have more than three full-time staff members.

In the accompanying table (see Table 9), staff analysis of foundations has been cross-tabulated with the foundation's founding auspices and program. Among other aspects of foundation organization and staffing, the table suggests the not surprising conclusion that, within the study's universe, there is a high degree of correlation between supportive programs and foundations with little or no staff.

Because, as Chapter 1 will indicate, a relatively small group of foundations employ a high percentage of all administrators, it was thought necessary to make some distinction between the comparatively well-staffed foundations in the study's universe and those that have only one or two employees or none at all. The distinction was deemed to be desirable both for purposes of comparison in the study and to avoid statistical distortion. Thirty-five foundations were therefore set apart from all others and for purposes of the study were identified as "managerially advanced." The connotation of this phrase in this context, is that each of the foundations so identified has *at least three full-time administrators*. The phrase implies no judgment as to the quality of the administration or program of a foundation, whether included or excluded from the group of thirty-five. Sixteen of the thirty-five foundations have over $100 million in assets, seven have between $50 and $100 million, nine have between $10 and $50 million, and three

Table 9. Staff Analysis of Foundations in Study's Universe Classified as to Founding Auspices and Program

Staff Analysis	Family General Purpose	Family Supportive	Family Operating	Community	Company-Sponsored	Total
Trustee-operated—no staff	1	250	6	14	49	320
	3.3%	54.7%	14.6%	28.0%	61.3%	48.6%
Trustee-operated with minor assistance	0	119	5	14	12	150
	0.0%	26.0%	12.2%	28.0%	15.0%	22.8%
1–3 staff members	7	83	22	21	17	150
	23.3%	18.2%	53.7%	42.0%	21.2%	22.3%
Over 3 staff members	22	5	8	1	2	38
	73.4%	1.1%	19.5%	2.0%	2.5%	5.8%
Total	30	457	41	50	80	658*
	4.5%	69.5%	6.2%	7.6%	12.2%	100.0%

* Information was not available on four foundations.

have under $10 million. Twenty-two are family general purpose foundations, eight are family supportive, two are family operating, two are community foundations, and one is a company-sponsored foundation. For obvious reasons, the thirty-five foundations are not identified. It can be said, however, that the list includes all the well-known, staffed foundations and a number of less well-known foundations that also qualify for inclusion because of the size of their staff.

Finally, the study's universe of foundations has been classified according to location. Table 10 which follows indicates the distribution of these

Table 10. Distribution of Study's Universe of Foundations According to Region

Geographical Region	Number Foundations	Percentage
Northeast	300	45.4
Southeast	62	9.4
North Central	174	26.3
South Central	69	10.4
West	56	8.5
Total	661	100.0%

foundations among the regions into which the country has been divided.[9] This table is supplemented by a cross-tabulation of location and asset classification of foundations (see Table 11). It confirms what most observers would anticipate, namely, that the wealthiest foundations in the study's universe (seven of the eleven largest foundations) are located in the states of the Northeast region, which includes New York City. The same regional concentration holds for other foundations falling into the remaining major asset categories, the Northeast, including New York City, exceeding the total for all the rest of the country or at least of any other region. Thus, eleven of the twenty-one foundations in the asset class, $100–$300 million, and fifty-two of the ninety-two foundations in the asset class $25–$100 million, are also located in the Northeast region. At the same time it may be worth noting that the states of the North Central region have the other four of the eleven very largest foundations in the study's universe and a goodly representation of foundations in every other asset class. There is, moreover, at least one foundation of considerable size—$100–$300 million—in every region into which the country has been divided.

The Administrator Career Questionnaire

From the data supplied by the study's foundation questionnaire and from allied sources, it was possible to compile a list of foundation executives to whom were sent individually addressed questionnaires concerning their service in foundations and their opinions on such service. These career questionnaires were mailed to 718 individuals. Four hundred and twenty-two, or 59 percent, completed and returned the questionnaire. About 10 percent of these had retired from the foundation field or taken other employment. The remaining respondents are employees of 124 foundations which, as will be noted in Chapter 1, are 59 percent of all foundations that employ at least one full-time executive (212) or 36 percent of all foundations that employ full-time and/or part-time executives (345).[10]

A few of these respondents probably painted a somewhat rosier picture of foundation service than their experience warranted. Others may have slanted the picture toward the more pessimistic side. Bias certainly cannot be ruled out. It is possible, moreover, that some respondents felt restricted by the questionnaire itself. For them, the right questions may not have been asked, or the questions may have been placed in the wrong context or formulated in such a way as to preclude a reasonably complete reply. Some, too,

---

[9] See Figure I for distribution of states into five regions.

[10] For further details on these 422 respondents to the career questionnaire, see Chapter 6.

Table 11. Geographical Location of Foundations of Various Asset Sizes in Study's Universe

Asset Ranges of Foundations	North-east	New York City*	South-east	North Central	South Central	West	Total
Under $1 million	21 7.0%	13 8.1%	5 8.1%	17 9.8%	6 8.7%	4 7.1%	53 8.0%
$1–$9.9 million	134 44.5%	66 41.0%	28 45.2%	91 52.3%	39 56.5%	27 48.2%	319 48.2%
$10–$24.9 million	76 25.2%	40 24.8%	17 27.4%	42 24.1%	13 18.8%	18 32.2%	166 25.1%
$25–$99.9 million	52 17.3%	32 19.9%	10 16.1%	16 9.2%	8 11.6%	6 10.7%	92 13.9%
$100–$299.9 million	11 3.7%	5 3.1%	2 3.2%	4 2.3%	3 4.4%	1 1.8%	21 3.2%
$300 million–$1 billion	6 2.0%	4 2.5%	0 0.0%	4 2.3%	0 0.0%	0 0.0%	10 1.4%
Over $1 billion	1 0.3%	1 0.6%	0 0.0%	0 0.0%	0 0.0%	0 0.0%	1 0.2%
Total	301 45.5%	161 24.3%	62 9.4%	174 26.3%	69 10.4%	56 8.4%	662 100.0%

* Although the figures for New York City are included in the figures for the Northeast, they are shown separately because of the heavy concentration of foundation wealth and activity in New York City.

may have experienced concern that their replies would not be treated confidentially, even though the study's directors promised that strictest secrecy would be observed.

Nevertheless, whatever the imperfections, these are valuable data. They reflect the views of a respectably large segment of the entire universe of foundation administrators and of the most articulate and most influential segment of the universe. Because of these data the study has been able to acquire an understanding of the foundation administrator's job—its opportunities, its rewards, and its liabilities—that is quite without precedent as respects scope and degree of accuracy. The details on how these administrators view foundations and foundation service appear in Chapter 6.

The Study's Data File

Thus the data file of the study includes two major sources of information, that is, data on 662 foundations secured by means of an institutional questionnaire and by other means previously described, and data on 422 foundation administrators secured through a questionnaire. In addition, a continuous dialogue was maintained with executives of various types of foundations, with the Council on Foundations, and, as already noted, with officials of The Foundation Center. Information and counsel were also received from the members of the study's distinguished advisory committee, whose names appear in the Preface.

These resulting rich and varied data, both institutional and personal, possibly the only data file of its kind in the world, were coded for the computer. Thus coded, the study has had the opportunity of providing not only a much more generous number of summary statistics (frequency tabulations) than is possible manually, but also some cross-tabulation that offer insights into the impact of such impersonal influences as environment and history on foundation administration and the foundation administrator.

Additional information on the contributions that others have made to this study will be found in the Preface. The Appendix contains reproductions of the two questionnaires and recapitulates data that, although relevant to the study, were not thought to be technically acceptable for analysis. They are reproduced in the Appendix for whatever interest and value they may have for the reader.

1

The Extent of Foundation Staffing—Absence of Staffing Policies

In a country that sets such store by managerial skills in its business structure as does the United States, it is something of a paradox that extension of these skills to nonprofit enterprise has been so slow. Full-time, professionally trained, and properly rewarded executive leadership and adequate staffing in administrative posts have only recently been accepted in the nation's universities, colleges, hospitals, and similar institutions. Many of even these organizations continue to rely for administrative tasks on their operating or professional staffs or upon their boards of trustees or other volunteers.

The American private foundation has been particularly backward. Whereas its sibling institutions may be said to have reached the Bronze Age in administrative staffing, the foundation has hardly reached the Stone Age. Indeed, among foundations, acceptance of the concept of administrative staffing is still so tentative that the total number of individuals who derive their livelihood and professional satisfactions from full-time employment in any foundation post above the clerical level is considerably less than the number of foundations. Data supplied to the study indicate that the number of such full-time employees is 1,012, of whom 840 are male and 172 female. These administrators are employed by 212 foundations. The authors are confident that the census they conducted did not overlook more than fifty full-time executive-level employees; hence, 1,062 is a generous estimate of all persons thus employed.

In addition to the full-time personnel, reports made to the study indicate that there are also some 349 part-time employees of foundations, other than consultants, above the clerical level.[1] If these are added to full-time personnel, the total comes to 1,411 individuals actually employed and compensated for devoting their energies and talents to the administrative and program activities of all American foundations. And if one adds the foundations that employ only part-time help to those that employ full-time help, the number of employing foundations rises from 212 to 345. How minuscule these numbers are becomes apparent when one compares them with the estimated total of foundations. If the previously mentioned figure of 24,000 is used as the estimated total, the staffed foundations do not exceed 1.5 percent of all foundations.[2]

Distribution of such staff as exists among employing foundations is, moreover, decidedly uneven. Of the 1,062 full-time administrators, approximately 25 percent are employed by a single foundation, namely, the Ford Foundation. About 15 percent serve The Rockefeller Foundation, the second largest foundation employer. Another 12 percent make up the administrative and program staffs of eleven other well-known foundations. These are the Carnegie Corporation, and the Commonwealth, Danforth, Duke, Houston, Kellogg, Kettering, R. K. Mellon, Mott, Rockefeller Brothers, and Sloan foundations or funds. Thus, these thirteen major foundations employ about half (52 percent) of all full-time personnel of executive stature serving foundations in the United States.[3]

With the exception of twenty-five or so part-time executives also employed by these thirteen foundations, the remaining full-time and part-time administrators, somewhat less than 60 percent of the total of 1,400, like the lonely hydrogen atoms in space, are dispersed among the remaining 332 foundations that this study has determined actually employ someone of executive stature either on a full-time or part-time basis. Astronomers and physicists have suggested that the hydrogen atoms in space are not quite so lonely as they were once deemed to be, but paid executives among these 332 foundations remain distinctly isolated. One hundred seventy-six individ-

---

[1] Reports on part-time executives are not as complete as are figures on full-time executives.

[2] The modest total of foundation administrators identified by the study suggests that the estimate of the recently published Peterson Commission report, namely that ". . . full-time professional personnel for all foundations probably does not exceed a few thousand" is too generous. The same observation might be made of that report's estimate that one-fifth of all foundations had paid staff. (See *Report and Recommendations of the Commission on Foundations and Private Philanthropy*, Chicago, Ill.: University of Chicago Press, 1970, p. 87.)

[3] The actual totals at the time the study took the census were as follows: Ford, 262; Rockefeller, 160; the other eleven foundations, 127.

uals occupy the single full-time or part-time staff positions existing in as many foundations. Seventy-five foundations employ two persons, and sixty-five foundations employ from three to five. The following tables show the distribution of six ranges of staff size for all executives, full-time and part-time, and for full-time executives only.

Figure II graphically portrays the distorted character of the distribution of full-time foundation staff above the clerical level among employing foundations. Using another analogy from space, it could be said that in the matter of staffing, the Ford Foundation has the relative magnitude of Jupiter, The Rockefeller Foundation that of the planet Saturn, with the remaining foundations employing full-time staff equating with some of the remaining planets and especially with the asteroids.

Table 12. Number of Foundations Employing Full-Time and/or Part-Time Executive-Level Staff and Classification According to the Number Employed

Ranges of Staff	Number of Foundations
1	176
2	75
3–5	65
6–10	17
11–100*	10
Over 100	2
Total foundations	345
(Total staff	1,361)

* The maximum for any foundation in this range does not exceed 40.

Table 13. Number of Foundations Employing Full-Time Executive-Level Staff and Classification According to the Number Employed

Ranges of Staff	Number of Foundations
1	113
2	40
3–5	38
6–10	11
11–100*	8
Over 100	2
Total foundations	212
(Total staff	1,012)

* The maximum for any foundation in this range does not exceed 40.

Figure II. Distribution of Full-Time Executive-Level Staff in Thirteen Relatively Well-Staffed Foundations and in All Other Foundations Employing Full-Time Executive-Level Staff

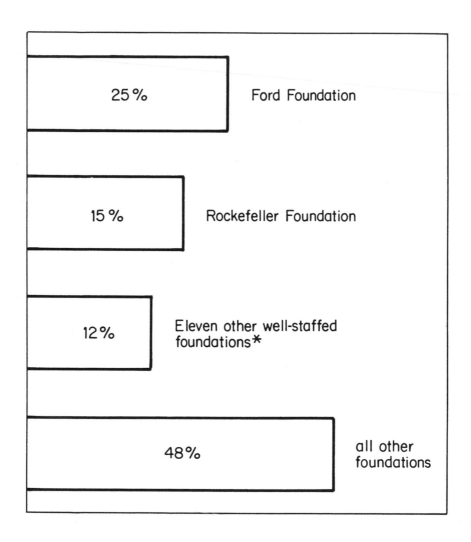

* As indicated in the text these eleven foundations are: Carnegie Corporation and the Commonwealth, Danforth, Duke, Houston, Kellogg, Kettering, R. K. Mellon, Mott, Rockefeller Brothers, and Sloan foundations or funds.

Geographical distribution of this modest universe of 1,400-plus administrators reflects their uneven distribution among foundations, since the few foundations with sizable aggregates of such employees are likely to be in New York City. Thus, eight of the twelve foundations having over eleven staff members of executive stature are located in New York City, including, of course, the two foundations with staffs in excess of one hundred, the Rockefeller and Ford foundations. The more modestly staffed foundations, that is, those employing from three to ten executives, are also to be found chiefly in the Northeast (which includes New York City), there being forty-six foundations with staffs of that size in the Northeast, or ten more than in all the rest of the United States. As for foundations with one or two staff members, the Northeast region has only seventeen less than the total for the rest of the country. Foundations with no staff that are included in the study's universe total 129 for the Northeast, which is 58 less than the number of unstaffed foundations in the other four regions into which the country has been divided (see Table 14).

As respects foundations in the study's universe other than the 345 which have been identified as having paid staff, responsibility for operations is usually assumed by the donor, persons closely connected with the donor, and trustees. Typically, the donor trustee or some representative of a founding family or corporation takes the nominal position of president or chairman. Other trustees, who may be relatives, business or professional associates, or employees of the donor, assume other positions in the executive hierarchy—vice president, secretary, treasurer, or gradations of these offices. Few such "officers" devote more than a fraction of their time to the affairs of the foundation—anywhere from 5 to 25 percent being typical. Normally such service is voluntary and unpaid, but the donor president or a trustee officer sometimes enjoys a salary. Moreover, under the terms of a trust, or judicially sanctioned administration of a trust, individual trustees in these foundations are frequently the recipients of fees.

Occasionally, a foundation without hired help is served by consultants, who may or may not be paid, and by compensated auditors, lawyers, investment counsellors, and other specialists. Sometimes, for a fee, such a foundation may be operated by the trust department of a bank or even by another foundation. For this study, the distinguishing characteristic of all such foundations is the absence of a single full-time or even part-time person of executive stature responsible for the foundation's operation, or some phase of its operation. For want of a more appropriate term, these foundations, as suggested in the Introduction, may be described as "trustee-operated."

In the following table, staffing is analyzed for the study's entire universe of foundations which are classified by asset size. Nearly half (48 per-

Table 14. Distribution of Staffed Foundations by Approximate Number of Staff and Geographical Region

Number of Executives	North- east	New York City*	Southeast	North Central	South Central	West	Total
None	129	67	28	98	34	27	316
	43.0%	41.6%	45.2%	56.3%	49.3%	48.2%	47.8%
1–2	117	56	26	56	27	25	251
	39.0%	34.8%	41.9%	32.2%	39.1%	44.6%	38.0%
3–10	46	30	7	18	8	3	82
	15.3%	18.6%	11.3%	10.4%	11.6%	5.4%	12.4%
Over 11	8	8	1	2	0	1	12
	2.7%	5.0%	1.6%	1.1%	0.0%	1.8%	1.8%
Total	300	161	62	174	69	56	661**
	45.4%		9.4%	26.3%	10.4%	8.5%	100.0%

* Although the figures for New York City are included in the figures for the Northeast, they are shown separately because of the heavy concentration of foundation wealth and activity in New York City.
** The record of one foundation was miscoded and therefore not included in this table. For map showing regional divisions in the United States, see p. 8.

Table 15. Number of Full-Time and Part-Time Executives According to the Asset Range of Foundations

Number of Executives	Under $1 million	$1–$9.9 million	$10–$24.9 million	$25–$99.9 million	$100–$299.9 million	$300 million—$1 billion	More than $1 billion	Total
None	25	159	94	32	6	1	0	317
	46.3%	49.8%	55.6%	34.8%	28.6%	11.1%	0.0%	47.9%
1	19	96	33	21	6	1	0	176
	35.2%	30.1%	19.9%	22.8%	28.6%	11.1%	0.0%	26.6%
2	4	36	22	11	1	1	0	75
	7.4%	11.3%	13.3%	12.0%	4.8%	11.1%	0.0%	11.3%
3–5	6	21	13	22	2	1	0	65
	11.1%	6.6%	7.8%	23.9%	9.5%	11.1%	0.0%	9.8%
6–10	0	5	3	4	4	1	0	17
	0.0%	1.6%	1.3%	4.3%	19.0%	11.1%	0.0%	2.6%
11–100	0	2	1	2	2	3	0	10
	0.0%	0.6%	0.6%	2.2%	9.5%	33.4%	0.0%	1.5%
Over 100	0	0	0	0	0	1	1	2
	0.0%	0.0%	0.0%	0.0%	0.0%	11.1%	100.0%	0.3%
Total	54	319	166	92	21	9	1	662
	8.2%	48.2%	25.0%	13.9%	3.2%	1.4%	0.1%	100.0%

cent) are trustee-operated, that is, without any paid staff, and more than 26 percent have but a single staff member. It is of interest to note that seven of the foundations without staff have assets of $100 million or more, and that 126 foundations without staff have assets between $10 and $100 million. There are also seven foundations with assets exceeding $100 million with only a single staff member.

Traditional Constraints on Staffing

It would require something more than analysis of the empirical data of this study to provide a reasonably definitive explanation as to why the staffing of foundations has not proceeded more rapidly and why foundations are so far behind even the relatively slow pace of other eleemosynary institutions. Such an explanation would require excursions into the history of philanthropy and into the nation's value system, social structure, and behavior, of a scope that the study is not equipped to undertake. Nevertheless, some clues as to the influences that have inhibited staffing among foundations may be gleaned from the limited data that the study has collected and from the observations of the study's directors.

One of the more important of such clues is related to the origin of a foundation. Of the entire national universe of 24,000 foundations, it is conservatively estimated that some 91 percent are of family-donor origin.[4] When first established, the foundation is usually regarded as a mere institutional conduit for the family's charities. In paying out its modest donations, there is no discernible need for assistance or counsel other than that supplied by the amateurs who operate the foundation. This administrative condition characterizes the great bulk of foundations with a family origin, many of which have assets of less than $100,000 and, in even more cases, of less than $50,000. Foundations of this size obviously cannot afford a paid staff and probably do not need it.

It happens, however, that this amateur administrative tradition often persists and becomes a habit even though many foundations, over the years, greatly increase their assets and the volume of their largesse. Growth rarely suggests that the family representative or trustee should give way to the paid administrator. Undoubtedly, this is a principal reason why the vast majority of family-derived foundations—despite the magnitude of the assets of many—continue without benefit of paid managerial or program staff.

A similar rejection of professional staffing persists among foundations with non-family origins. In company-sponsored foundations, employees

---

[4] This percentage is derived from information supplied by The Foundation Center. The 9 percent of foundations not classified as having family-donor origin are an estimated 2,000 company-sponsored foundations and an estimated 250 community foundations.

of the founding business serve as trustees and devote such time as may be required to the affairs of the foundation. Even when such a foundation becomes reasonably wealthy in its own right, and one or two individuals are employed full-time by the foundation, the employees are usually former company executives, often retired or about to be retired. Usually they are not independent foundation "careerists," although there are examples of thoroughly capable and expert heads of company-sponsored foundations.

Similarly, in the case of the community foundation, created to distribute philanthropic funds to a city or other local area, bank officers who, as trustees, control such funds, and civic leaders who serve on a "distribution committee" to advise the bankers have in the past usually been deemed sufficient to operate the foundation. It should be noted, however, that in community foundations, professional employees are currently becoming more usual.

The following table identifies the staffing (and non-staffing) practices of the foundations that are included in the study, the foundations being classified this time according to their auspices, or origin, and their program (see Table 16). It will be noted that it is the family-supportive, community, and company-sponsored foundations that account for a large percentage of non-staffed and meagrely staffed foundations.

Table 16. Number of Full-Time and Part-Time Executives According to the Auspices and Program of the Foundation

Number of Executives	Family General Purpose	Family Supportive	Family Operating	Community	Company-Sponsored	Total
None	0	247	11	15	42	315
	0.0%	53.9%	26.8%	30.0%	52.5%	47.8%
1	1	122	9	21	22	175
	3.3%	26.6%	22.0%	42.0%	27.5%	26.5%
2	3	51	6	8	7	75
	10.0%	11.2%	14.6%	16.0%	8.8%	11.4%
3–5	10	34	9	5	7	65
	33.3%	7.4%	22.0%	10.0%	8.8%	9.9%
6–10	9	3	3	1	1	17
	30.0%	0.7%	7.3%	2.0%	1.3%	2.6%
11–100	5	1	3	0	1	10
	16.7%	0.2%	7.3%	0.0%	1.2%	1.5%
Over 100	2	0	0	0	0	2
	6.7%	0.0%	0.0%	0.0%	0.0%	0.3%
Total	30	458	41	50	80	659*
	4.6%	69.5%	6.2%	7.6%	12.1%	100.0%

* In three cases, it was not possible to ascertain auspices.

Another possible reason for the willingness of foundations to operate without paid staff is the belief of many philanthropists that donors and their advisors can be as creative with their philanthropy as any paid specialist. Proponents of this viewpoint cite examples of families and individuals who have used their largesse creatively, either directly or through a foundation they created. The Medicis are a case in point. Members of that family, or some of them at least, were gifted philanthropists. They patronized and encouraged talent in the arts, and for this, the world is forever in their debt. The Rothschilds are another example. In the United States in more recent times, one can point to the elder Rockefeller and his son and even to the third to bear the family founder's name. The roster can be extended to include Andrew Carnegie, Julius Rosenwald, Alfred P. Sloan, Jr., Daniel Guggenheim and his son, Harry F. Guggenheim, Robert Lehmann, and many others. It can be persuasively argued that probably no professionally staffed foundation could have used the resources of these individuals more constructively than they did themselves. But because such "amateurs" made an enviable record as philanthropists, they have helped to strengthen the notion that professional philanthropic administrators can be dispensed with.

These amateur stars of philanthropy have also helped to fortify, at least morally, another practice that makes professional foundation administrators virtually superfluous. This is the practice of creating trust indentures to carry out a founder's wishes after his death—*mortmain* with a vengeance. The trustees who act as the testator's surrogate have clear directions as to philanthropic policy and the identity of beneficiaries: they consequently discern no need for hired help to carry on the foundation program. And they are quite right. Staff people, especially program staff people, are not necessary because all the philanthropic thinking has been done and its results are enforceable by the terms of the indenture.

In many cases of this kind, the trustees are the recipients of handsome fees under the terms of the trust. These fees provide a reinforcing argument, if any were needed, for trustee operation of the foundation, since the trustees want to earn their fee. Some of the wealthiest foundations in America operate in this fashion. About the only employees of executive rank whom they may require are controllers and, possibly, investment counsellors.

"Dead-hand" administration of a foundation may exert an inhibitory influence on staffing even when the dead hand has not been institutionalized in an indenture. In many cases, trustees and their advisors feel morally committed to carrying out what they believe to be the departed donor's charitable objectives even though he may not have sanctified them in a founding instrument. The idea of a paid administrator is regarded with suspicion because of the belief that the administrator will use his influence to change the program objectives of the donor. Even more deplorable, in the opinion of those who want to preserve a departed donor's influence on a foundation, is the alleged tendency of "strange" people, brought in to run a foundation, to promote values and ideologies wholly at variance with those espoused by the founder. It is difficult to estimate how pervasive such suspicions of professional philanthropists may actually be, but to the extent that they exist, they discourage the acquisition of paid staff.

Taken together, restraints on staffing such as these are probably of less significance than one other factor. This is the absence, among the great majority of foundations, of a philanthropic program that requires specialized knowledge of philanthropy and the capacity to identify high priority social and cultural objectives—needs that a trained, paid, staff person would presumably satisfy. As already indicated, a few donor-controlled foundations have, in the past, displayed progressive and innovative thinking about the use of their resources. But the same cannot be said of the vast majority of foundations, whether operated by the donor or his family, or by trustees, with or without instructions from the donor.

By and large, all such foundations tend to support the conventional and the *status quo*, that is, they direct their resources toward the support of established charities and eleemosynary institutions. Indeed, a similar observation may be made of foundations with some paid staff and occasionally of foundations with relatively sizable staffs. More than 68 percent of the foundations included in the study's universe indicated that their operations are purely "supportive"; and this figure is raised to approximately 90 percent if those foundations are added that combine, with supportive grants, provision for some project or projects that the foundation itself administers or for programs that combine innovative and supportive projects.

The vast majority of foundations thus concede they are wholly or partly engaged in the socially laudable but distinctly conventional subsidization and support of churches, universities, museums, and local charities of all sorts, or that they are supporting prizes, scholarships, fellowships, and other grants to individuals. Occasionally, to be sure, these latter grants may be unusual in their purpose in that they focus on the creation of some new skill or insight. Normally, they constitute run-of-the-mill assistance for scholarly training, travel, writing, and research. Of the total engaged wholly or partly in these supportive activities, close to one-half (236 of 517) have no staff, and about one-third (151 of 517) have one staff person. Of the balance, sixty-one have a staff of two persons; fifty, of from three to five; and nineteen, of six or more.

Only occasionally does a foundation without staff or with only limited staff claim that it is exercising any serious initiative in designing studies, demonstrations, or unusual projects to gain new knowledge, or that it is assisting or supporting unorthodox causes or ideas. When it does so, it usually asserts that it combines supportive philanthropy with such innovative philanthropy. About 15 percent of the reporting foundations characterize their programs as this combination. On the other hand, most foundations employing five or more staff persons identify their program as a combination of supportive and innovative philanthropy with, in some cases, direct operation of certain projects. Of the twenty-seven foundations with a full-time staff of more than five persons—about 5 percent of all foundations that reported on program—only five said that they were purely supportive. The affinity of unstaffed foundations for supportive programs is thus reasonably clear (even though three of the unstaffed group stated that they are directing all their funds to innovative projects), as is the tendency of the more generously staffed foundations to move in the opposite or more innovative program direction. Table 17 provides the pertinent statistics.

Thus the evidence collected by the study fortifies the observation made earlier that the type of program supported by the vast majority of foundations discourages staffing because that program does not appear to require it. The characteristic type of program of the American foundation is supportive, and the foundation is basically what we have previously labeled a conduit type of philanthropic organization. To administer such a program for such a foundation requires relatively little expertise. Certainly, it does not take much philanthropic knowledge and administrative competence to hand money over the counter to well-known applicants from the eleemosynary fraternity. With a few consultants and possibly one or two minor employees, many foundation trustees or other amateurs feel themselves quite able to take care of those program demands. Other foundations, often possessing considerable wealth, which support such a program, feel that they can get along with one or two people of executive stature. Whether this is the kind of philanthropy which foundations should dispense may be open to debate; but so long as they do dispense it, there will be little movement toward more generous staffing.

Undoubtedly, constraints against staffing such as have just been reviewed are among the principal reasons for the low level of total staff of American foundations. Individually, or in combination, they explain or help to justify the unwillingness of donors or trustees to acquire paid help of stature or even to concede that such help would be desirable. Moreover, little evidence was unearthed by the study to suggest that these anti-staffing influences are losing their sway over the foundation community. To be sure, thirty-four foundations indicated that they had acquired their first full-time administrator within the previous four years, and four indicated that they contemplated making such a move within the following year, but the number of foundations having taken or contemplating this kind of action is more than matched by those who said they were satisfied to operate

Table 17. Number of Full-Time and Part-Time Executives According to the Type of Program of the Foundation

Number of Executives	Supportive	Initiating, Designing, etc	Operating	Supportive and Initiating/Designing	Supportive and Operating	Initiating/Designing and Operating	Combination all three types program	Total
None	213 55.6%	3 50.0%	6 27.3%	11 13.3%	11 31.4%	1 6.7%	1 6.3%	246 43.9%
1	98 25.6%	1 16.7%	4 18.2%	39 47.0%	8 22.9%	0 0.0%	6 37.5%	156 27.9%
2	35 9.1%	1 16.7%	4 18.2%	14 16.9%	9 25.7%	3 20.0%	3 18.7%	69 12.3%
3–5	32 8.4%	1 16.6%	6 27.3%	12 14.5%	5 14.3%	5 33.3%	1 6.3%	62 11.1%
6–10	3 0.8%	0 0.0%	2 9.0%	3 3.6%	2 5.7%	3 20.0%	2 12.5%	15 2.6%
11–100	2 0.5%	0 0.0%	0 0.0%	3 3.6%	0 0.0%	2 13.3%	3 18.7%	10 1.8%
Over 100	0 0.0%	0 0.0%	0 0.0%	1 1.2%	0 0.0%	1 6.7%	0 0.0%	2 0.4%
Total	383 68.3%	6 1.1%	22 3.9%	83 14.8%	35 6.3%	15 2.7%	16 2.9%	560* 100.0%

* It was not possible to obtain program data on the remaining 102 foundations in the study's universe.

as they have been operating and see no need for staff. Unsolicited comments like the following were frequent: "We have no need for paid staff"; "No paid staff in grant-making operations—the donor handles all grants."

The reaction of the bulk of the unstaffed foundations to the study's questionnaire is itself revealing on this question of the foundations' attitude toward staff. A large percentage simply ignored the questionnaire. A few sent a letter consisting of two or three simple sentences announcing that the foundation was not giving out information of the type requested. Others behaved somewhat like the prisoner of war who had been instructed to reveal to his captors only his name, rank, and serial number.

It is probable that the penchant for secrecy, endemic with foundations, explains in part the failure to respond or the curtness of many of the responses that were made. But in most instances the chief reason for the failure to communicate seems to have been the absence of any staff above the rank of clerk who could write a letter and convey information with some authority. Nor did the foundations involved appear to realize this fact. One or two admitted that they did not have the time to compile the information, and one family head of a well-known foundation said that he was too busy making grants to provide the kind of information the study requested. But in these and other cases, no indication was given that the foundations were prepared to remedy these inadequacies. It may be possible to defend the absence of staff in some foundations, especially small foundations; but it would be difficult to convince an objective observer that a foundation of any size can operate effectively without at least one or two employees of stature capable of explaining the foundation's programs and policies to the public.

Absence of Staffing Policies

With personnel so limited, it is probably to be expected that the foundation constituency would have given little thought to staffing policy or to what the more academically minded would identify as personnel administration. At any rate, there is virtually no evidence of formal thinking by foundations about the optimum size of staff in a particular organization, about staff recruitment, about the quality and substance of staff training, and about the responsibilities individual staff members of various grades should assume within a foundation's organizational structure. Neither, apparently, has much consideration been given to increasing staff productivity by familiarizing new staff members with their duties or providing appropriate in-service training for new staff members or for staff assigned to new duties.

Similarly, professional standards that might influence salary levels, salary review practices, fringe benefits, and the like, are nonexistent. To all such matters the foundation community has given little thought. Thus, for example, not one of the last five annual public reports of each of a half dozen of the most advanced foundations examined by the study had anything to say about staff matters other than making routine announcements of appointments, transfers, promotions, retirements, and deaths. It is likely, moreover, that even if the researcher were made privy to the minutes of board, committee, or staff meetings, he would encounter no discussion in depth about staffing. Except as respects the changing status of particular individuals already employed or to be employed, the subject rarely if ever appears on the agenda.

Inability to repair to any standard source of information on staff matters was tacitly admitted during the course of the study. Its questionnaire had hardly been dispatched to the foundations before many of them began to make inquiries about the personnel data which, it was presumed, the completed questionnaires would reveal. Information was sought about customary salaries for foundation officers of various levels of responsibility, about practices among foundations concerning fringe benefits, about the proper relations of staff and trustees, and about the qualities to be sought in candidates for various kinds of foundation responsibility. The relative frequency of these inquiries and the expectation that the questionnaire data would supply answers provided rather startling confirmation of the lack of professional guidelines or standards for foundation staffing practices.

There are minor exceptions to this otherwise *tabula rasa* of foundation discussion on staffing. They consist of an occasional nugget of opinion extracted from the biography of a philanthropist, an isolated chapter in one of the infrequent commentaries on foundations, and the appraisal or restructuring of program in which one or two foundations occasionally engage and sometimes publish. An example of the latter, which the study consulted, is the so-called Gaither Committee report on the Ford Foundation. The report was issued in November 1949, by a committee of distinguished scholars, philanthropists, and administrators, headed by the late H. Rowan Gaither, a lawyer, and subsequently head of the foundation. The committee had been asked to plan the organization and implementation of the foundation following its receipt of sizable funds from the estates of Edsel and Henry Ford. Having formulated a program for the foundation that, in the committee's opinion, "had considerable homogeneity and focus," the committee proceeded to make recommendations as to the kind of people who might put that program into effect.

The half dozen principal officers of the foundation, said the committee, should "be men of broad experience and general interests"; and "far more emphasis should be put on general interests and ability to deal with all kinds of people, and on a deep conviction with respect to the fundamental objectives of the program, than on technical or specialized ability in any one of the sciences." In recommending the employment of such "generalists," the Gaither Committee felt that it was strongly supported by the careers of Abraham Flexner and Wickliffe Rose. Flexner, whose investigations, financed by a Carnegie grant, did so much for medical education, and Rose, who greatly influenced public-health policies during his tenure with the Rockefeller interests, were respectively a "layman" and a "philosopher" and had no technical training in the fields on which they left so deep an impress.

As to staff members, the committee felt that no definite rules could be laid down for recruitment and tenure. It counseled against haste in making tenure appointments. The proper procedure, it suggested, would be to make temporary appointments of people on leave from other positions. It also suggested that staff be recruited not only from the field of education but also from business, government, and journalism. For any specialized service it recommended temporary employment of experts as consultants rather than additions to permanent staff.

In commenting on salary policy, it proposed one high enough to recruit "the best men from universities, government, and non-profit institutions, without being so high as to block entirely any possibility of movement in the opposite direction." If the salary policy should exclude some of the abler men, that fact would have to be accepted, said the committee, because economic rewards alone could not be allowed to be the dominant motive for foundation service. Such rewards, it insisted, must be supplemented by a "strong desire for public service and a strong interest in the Foundation's program."[6]

The Gaither Committee's primary concern was program and not staffing. The latter was an incidental concern and properly so. Some of the report's shortcomings as a discussion of staffing are therefore understandable. In any event, its value as such a discussion is limited. Its observations are often highly generalized and rather superficial. Its tone is also somewhat pietistic or, at any rate, reverential toward the foundation constituency's hitherto accepted ideas on staffing—such as they were. The report also concerns a foundation that is not exactly typical. Nevertheless, with all its shortcomings, it is the most extended discussion of staffing published by a foundation that the study's directors encountered and the only one that could be dignified by the term "discussion." The existence of this not too fertile oasis of foundation concern about staffing, in what is otherwise a desert, underscores the observation that began this discussion, namely,

---

[6] For these excerpts see *Report of the Study for The Ford Foundation on Policy and Program*, Detroit, Michigan, 1949, pp. 133–135.

that foundations have indulged in little or no systematic thinking about staffing and that formal discussions on the subject are virtually nonexistent.

It thus becomes difficult to quell the suspicion that, even among those relatively few foundations that have paid staff, appointments are rarely made in accordance with formally established managerial requirements. Normally, staff has simply accumulated, *ad hoc*, as resources grew, or program changed or expanded, or the writ of the donor which, as a matter of course, usually frowns on staff expansion, lost its persuasive influence. This observation applies even to the half dozen most advanced foundations. As already noted, there is virtually no evidence of advance planning about staff and little thought about goals and program and the staff needed to implement them over the long term. Certainly there is little, if any, discussion about the usual concerns of personnel management.

A review of foundation staffing such as is contemplated in this study must therefore rely almost wholly upon the empirical data supplied by foundations and administrators. Most of these data are necessarily cast in quantitative terms. Fortunately, in supplying these data many of those who were queried and who responded supplemented them with extensive comment of an interpretive nature. Such comment, therefore, provides an excellent subjective antidote for what might otherwise tend to become an almost purely quantitative analysis of staffing practices.

Influence of the Tax Reform Act of 1969

There are those who hope that some of the recent social and legal pressure on foundations, notably the various congressional investigations and the tax reform legislation in which those investigations culminated at the end of 1969, may eventually force all unstaffed foundations, and particularly the larger ones, to look with greater favor upon some degree of full-time staffing. Hope is also expressed that these outside pressures may compel foundations with staff, especially those with staffs of some size, to give more attention than in the past to constructive staffing policies. Such foundations, it is suggested, may want to structure internal management to accommodate staff people of diverse talents and training, give increased attention to matching preparation with the demands of the prospective foundation assignment and, by identifying socially more daring and more imaginative program challenges, attract more competent and more dedicated staffs. In short, hope is expressed that more foundations will forego *ad hoc* staffing policies in favor of something more systematic.

The possibility of such constructive developments exists, at least in part, as a result of these governmental pressures. At any rate, as will be noted later,[7] foundation personnel whom the study's directors consulted are of the opinion that the 1969 tax legislation will increase the demand for lawyers, public relations experts, financial counsellors, and individuals skilled in business management. Foundations, it is contended, will seek individuals with these backgrounds in order to cope with the new governmental regulations. Moreover, evidence was supplied the study that appointments of such persons were being made, although the number who had been appointed was not impressive.

Alongside this potentially constructive personnel development looms another that is not so likely to win applause. A sizable number of respondents also feel that the pressure of the new legislation will discourage resort to more innovative and more daring programs because such programs could conceivably jeopardize a foundation's tax exemption or result in fines on foundation personnel. The result therefore, so say these more pessimistic respondents, may be a more cautious grant policy on the part of foundations—one that will be served by maintaining the traditional supportive or conduit type of philanthropy. Should this turn out to be the case, there would be little hope of more expansive or more expert staffing, at least in the program area, for foundations would normally persist with programs that traditionally have required virtually no expert staff or, indeed, no staff at all. At the same time, really outstanding and imaginative candidates for managerial and program staff might be disinclined to enter foundation service because programs lack challenge.

It is still too soon after the enactment of the 1969 legislation to express an opinion as to which of these conflicting trends will prevail. Clearly, expanded and more systematic staffing of foundations requires that existing social and legal pressures not be allowed to ally themselves with those traditional forces antagonistic to staffing canvassed earlier. Unless such an alliance is avoided, it is highly unlikely that the universe of foundation administrators will be expanded appreciably or that foundations will move to improve staffing policies. A major requirement for achieving such advances is that an increasing number of donors and trustees of foundations move from a conduit to a more project-oriented type of philanthropy. They are unlikely to move in this direction unless the social and governmental climate encourages them to do so—or at least does not discourage them. In the pages that follow, the opinion of the foundation community on these conflicting trends will be set forth in greater detail.

---

[7] See Chapter 6.

2

The Employment and
Specialization of Staff

Initial staffing by most foundations is frequently casual. Often a foundation's first move toward staffing is the hiring of an individual on a part-time basis to help guide the administrative, financial, and/or program aspects of its activities. The appointee, who may or may not be a member or friend of the founding family, may remain on a part-time basis over a period of years, or he may gradually assume full-time status as the assets and activities of the foundation increase.

In lieu of such an appointment, a very few small, family supportive, foundations begin staffing on a cooperative basis, an arrangement that is often suitable for foundations with kindred program interests and roughly similar endowments. They may feel that neither their assets nor their program needs require a full time staff person; nevertheless, they want professional help. Accordingly, they share an administrator with other foundations. Under this arrangement, the administrator gives all his time to his job, but allots a portion of it to each foundation, investigating programs and helping each foundation to prepare reports for their respective boards. In New York, the Joint Foundation Support, Inc., is an example of such an arrangement, and infrequently there appear to be somewhat similar arrangements elsewhere.

Another occasional answer to the administrative problem of the smaller foundation of the supportive type that cannot itself afford paid full-time or even part-time assistance is the practice of having one foundation manage another. Again, however, only one or two examples were uncovered. Other experiments in common or cooperative professional administration of small foundations may exist that were not reported, but the probable instances of such experiments are few and far between.[1]

Job Descriptions of Foundation Staff

Among the contingent of foundations in which there is only one paid person of executive stature, the individual is a kind of jack-of-all-trades. As shown in Chapter 1, 176 foundations reported that they employed only a single person on a full-time or part-time basis. Assuming the role of chief executive officer under a variety of titles, this single executive usually combines supervision of the foundation and duties relating to the board of trustees and the general public with certain financial duties and general program responsibility. Some of the specific functions of the chief executive of a one-staff family supportive foundation are set forth in Figure III.

Typically, the grants made by this kind of foundation are likely to be of the conventional kind—what in the study has been labeled supportive—that is, grants in support of the operation, or possibly the expansion and improvement of one or more established legal charities. Occasionally, the lone executive in such a foundation may assume responsibility for the administration of a permanent, quasi-internal, project, such as a scholarship or fellowship project that may or may not be the foundation's sole program activity.

The solitary foundation executive is a "generalist." He is a generalist as respects his foundation responsibilities, and he is probably a generalist in the qualifications he brings to his assignment. Undoubtedly, he is one reason why commentators on the foundation scene are so fond of the term "generalist" in identifying the kind of person who ideally should administer foundation philanthropy. A slight departure from this pattern may occur in the case of the occasional foundation that is largely or exclusively concerned with the direct operation of some charity or non-profit project, as, for example, a recreational or health program. In this case, the single foundation executive may well be an expert or professional practitioner in the field in which the foundation is active, instead of a generalist. He may also combine administrative functions with his professional contributions to the foundation's direct operations.

The extensive span of activity of the lone paid staff member of a family

---

[1] The community foundation should be credited with having been a pioneer in "cooperative" foundation administration. By segregating, and maintaining the individuality of, many local trusts, legacies, and other donations, the community foundation has made it unnecessary for donors to set up small family foundations. At the same time, where staffed, the community foundation has provided expert administration—something the donor could not have afforded had he set up his own family foundation.

Figure III. Functions of the Single Paid Executive Who Serves as Head of a Family Supportive Foundation

Trustee-Related Functions
Keeps trustees informed
Prepares reports for board
Prepares minutes of board
  meetings

*Information/Communica-
tion Functions*
Prepares annual report
Prepares financial report

Supervisory Functions
Secures and supervises
  office staff
Handles correspondence

Program Functions
Develops reviews of fields
  for grant policies
Designs projects
Directs programs
Carries out all detail work
  on grants:
    meeting and interview-
      ing applicants
    reviewing grant appli-
      cations
    making recommenda-
      tions to the trustees
    making grant payments
    following up and eval-
      uating projects

*Financial/Investment
  Functions (less important)*
Usually participates in these
  functions only to extent he
  maintains sufficient familiarity with investment and
  financial matters with which
  to prepare reports for board.
  (These functions are more apt
  to be put in the hands of
  professional money managers,
  of the board of trustees, of
  a single board member, or
  of a special finance and
  investment committee.)

foundation is also characteristic of a company-sponsored or a community foundation, which, if it has any paid executive staff at all, may limit itself to a single person who serves as head. In the community foundation, there is at least one additional function that it is peculiar to it that this person must discharge. This is fund-raising—soliciting gifts or encouraging bequests, promoting the use of the foundation to prospective donors, and generally increasing the philanthropic resources of the foundation. This special activity is perhaps only part of the community foundation's chief executive's role as interpreter of his foundation to the public, and of his role in maintaining liaison with local officials and leaders and using the foundation as a community resource for a variety of local organizations.

Foundations with a single paid staff person often continue to use the voluntary services of the donor family or organization or of trustees on which non-staffed foundations are dependent. Hence, a one-executive foundation may be only degrees removed from the typical trustee-operated foundation delineated earlier. Occasionally, too, such a foundation may eke out staff with consultants and possibly with one or two part-time employees of clerical stature.

Among foundations with one or two staff members canvassed in the study, approximately 20 percent indicated that these staff members were on a part-time basis. In general, part-time staff at various executive levels are found in family supportive foundations with relatively modest assets, in community foundations, and in company-sponsored foundations where most staff members divide their time between the donor firm and the foundation. The following table shows the ranges of professional time that forty-seven part-time executives reported giving to their respective foundations.

Table 18. Number of Part-Time Staff and Percentage of Time They Give to Foundation Work

Number	Percent
12	5–25
21	26–50
12	51–75
2	76–90

In foundations with from two to four paid executive staff members, the chief executive discharges many of the same duties as he does in a one-man organization, although he may spend more time on program initiation and development and in serving on executive or financial committees. Even when the paid staff of a foundation includes as many as five individuals of executive stature, the responsibilities of the chief executive do not change greatly. For him the shift is toward a greater degree of administrative responsibility for a larger operation. He gives more attention to planning the goals of the foundation and to supervising other staff members. Although at this stage of staffing, internal financial, secretarial, and logistic duties may, in large measure, be delegated or transferred to other employees, the chief executive continues to exercise broad supervisory powers over finances and investment, the presentation of recommendations to the board, review of grants, representation of the foundation to the public, and liaison work between the foundation and investment and legal advisors.

Indeed, the concept of combining administrative and program duties that characterizes meagerly staffed foundations often persists as the foundation increases staff. Thus, not only did the 176 foundations with a single staff person report such a combination, but so did twenty-five more with two-person staffs, six with three staff members, and eight with four. At least one foundation with eleven on its executive staff insisted that each individual divide his time between administrative and program responsibilities, and another foundation with seventeen staff persons reported a similar policy. The conclusion seems to be—and it is a conclusion buttressed by the opinion of many of the foundation executives reporting to the study—that however far removed from the program side of a foundation's activities a staff person may be, he likes to be involved in program functions if he can, because it is the foundation's activity in philanthropy that makes service in it meaningful and attractive.

With exceptions just noted, it is only in foundations that employ as many as six to ten persons of executive stature that one discovers the beginnings of a formal division of labor. In addition to the chief executive officer, there may be a deputy and at least the nucleus of a staff group who subsequently become exclusively or mainly concerned with program. Members of this staff group, called program officers, are key individuals in a foundation with heavy commitments to finance other institutions, individuals other than its own staff, and programs at least nominally under the management of other institutions.

In many ways the program officer satisfies the popular conception of the authentic foundation philanthropist. At any rate, he exerts a relatively wide and varied range of authority in handling grants. Included among his functions are the following:

——Evaluation and investigation of grant applications
——Recommendation on grants
——Design and development of grants and proposals
——Administration of programs in one or more (or all) of a foundation's areas of concern

——Monitoring and appraising projects and programs
——Supervising other program staff

Although concentrating on program, a number of program officer respondents mentioned certain budgetary, legal, and internal administrative tasks, and the handling of correspondence affecting grant proposals. In describing his job, one wrote ". . . mainly, though, I handle *mountains* of mail." Other program officers characterized their jobs in these terms: "Handle grant applications, negotiate proposals, write grant applications, and monitor grants. Also find new areas for grant making"; "Administer two programs and run sixteen conferences a year. Prepare requests and proposals for committee on higher education"; "Screen applications and interview applicants. Assist in preparation of annual and other reports."

Like other staff members, program officers have many titles, some of which may not do justice to their responsibilities. Indeed, the significance of a title may be inversely proportional to the title holder's degree of responsibility for making decisions. A vice president, for example, may have little responsibility as a program officer, whereas an executive associate, executive assistant, or even an associate, may be entrusted with the responsibilities of developing, managing, and monitoring a large program.

Whenever a foundation appoints its first program specialist or increases the number of persons concerned specifically with program, that kind of staffing seems to exert a catalytic influence in increasing the number of persons in the foundation's non-program areas. Rather quickly the foundation may acquire expert financial, secretarial, informational, and logistic staff. Thus, where it had previously found it possible to get along with a trustee committee on investment policy and outside financial counselors, the foundation may now proceed to appoint an internal officer to advise on investments, manage the portfolio, and execute investment decisions.[2] To relieve a lone secretarial officer of part of his duties, an internal auditor or accountant may be appointed. He takes over from the outside auditing firm that previously may have handled the day-to-day requirements of the foundation. The outside firm is thereafter limited to preparing the annual audit.

In a few cases, a director of reports and public information may also be added and possibly someone to supervise clerical personnel and general maintenance. Few foundations have yet employed a staff lawyer to serve as full-time legal counsel, and the addition has been recent in all cases. It

---

[2] In at least a few foundations, this process has been given an impetus, perhaps, by the regulations of the 1969 Tax Reform Act and by the decline in the stock market in 1970. At any rate, more foundations with considerable assets have begun to examine the return on their endowment and conclude that a higher rate might be obtained through the use of an individual full-time financial counselor.

would not be surprising if, in the coming decade, other foundations took this step to help interpret the legislation and rulings emanating from Washington.

Among perhaps a score of the thirty-five managerially advanced foundations singled out earlier, there is even clearer evidence of this kind of growing staff specialization. In these cases, financial, housekeeping, and logistic activities are placed in the hands of separate officers or groups of officers. Rudimentary departmentalization is also encountered in program areas. Thus, the Ford Foundation identifies five areas, each headed by a major executive. Somewhat similar structuring is found at Danforth, JDR 3rd Fund, Rockefeller, and Commonwealth. At other foundations such as Carnegie, Sloan, Kellogg, and Field, program areas may be identified but there is only an occasional internal administrative division based on a program area.

In foundations such as Russell Sage Foundation and Twentieth Century Fund, which conduct a good deal of in-house research and investigation in addition to making grants to outsiders, senior staff members may also be distinguished specialists in the field or fields in which the foundation is active. Again, they are likely to combine research in their speciality with supervisory activities. The latter may include advising the foundation on desirable candidates for grants and other program functions such as investigating grant applicants and evaluating grants. Occasionally, their responsibilities may slip over into certain internal managerial activities.

Foundations with wide-ranging international interests such as Ford, Rockefeller, and Kellogg, also have field program and managerial staffs, and if they conduct large-scale operations directly (as do Rockefeller and Ford), these field staffs include a good many distinguished scientists, economists, agronomists, sociologists, and others with special training and knowledge. Basically, these people are not administrators, nor even program staff in the sense in which the word "program" is normally used among grant-making foundations. Rather, they are operations people, that is, individuals who contribute the specialized knowledge required for the actual operation of a project. Even so, many of them are called upon to exercise supervisory responsibility over subordinate staff. Moreover, most of them commingle program skill with their research and operations, advising their respective foundations as to possible philanthropic opportunities in disciplinary areas in which they are knowledgeable.

Some of the most often mentioned functions of the field staff of the Ford Foundation outside the United States include the following:

——Developing, planning, and administering a program
——Formulating, recommending, and administering grants
——Monitoring existing projects and evaluating past projects
——Recruiting and supervising staff

——Managing the foundation's regional office or offices

——Acting as the foundation's representative in relations with the foreign government in which activities are being supported

In truth, many field representatives of the Ford Foundation have jobs that are comparable with those of chief executives of a medium size foundation in the United States.

In The Rockefeller Foundation, a field representative's functions include many of the same duties, with the addition of the direction or conduct of research. Several overseas representatives of this foundation mentioned relationships with a foreign university, with the representative assuming such roles as dean of agriculture, visiting professor, supervisor of theses, or some other teaching or administrative role in the foreign university.

In these project-oriented, general purpose foundations, the intimacy existing between the foundation's program staff and its projects is a reflection of the program staff's practice of taking the initiative in setting program goals, designing projects or programs (often sharing responsibility with prospective grantees), and of administering projects after they have been set up. These practices are especially prevalent outside the United States. In the absence of appropriate institutions and trained personnel, foundations seeking to advance the economy or social structure of a foreign community often find it necessary to involve program staff people more intimately, and for a longer term, in the operation of a project than would be the case in comparable domestic situations.

Staff-Trustee Relationship in Program Matters

A word might be inserted here about the respective roles of the staff and the trustees of managerially advanced foundations in determining the actual allocation of a foundation's grants. Usually the staff role includes not only initial study, screening of applications, and the recommendation of certain projects, but also extends to the formal decision-making process. Seventy-eight percent of the administrators who responded to the study's career questionnaire said they participated in staff decision-making meetings, and about half of these said they voted when a decision to reject or recommend a project was made by the staff. Senior program officers usually have the responsibility of appearing before the trustees to defend projects on the board's agenda or to make broad policy recommendations. Often, the foundation's chief executive officer is a member of the board, 135 foundations having reported to the study that this was the case.

Unquestionably, such prerogatives as the foregoing tend to preserve for the program staff and other staff the actual power of decision in the making of grants, since a board of trustees would usually hesitate to deny a recommendation that had been carefully screened by the staff as a whole and had been conscientiously investigated and convincingly presented. On the other hand, though a board customarily accedes to staff recommendations, such acquiescence takes place within the context of considerable formal and informal interaction between board and staff. The effect is to direct staff actions into areas and projects known to be within the purview of the foundation as established by the trustees.

Table 19. Percentage of Staff People Engaged in Various Activities Affecting Program and Program-Related Matters*

Activity	Percentage Engaged in Activity
Screening requests	78.2
Participating in staff or other decision-making meetings	78.2
Examining projects in depth	72.3
Making formal recommendations on broad policy matters as well as on projects	63.5
Appearing before the trustees to discuss grants or projects	59.2
Designing projects	53.1
Directing or helping to operate projects	36.7
Voting in staff meetings	36.5
Making final decision on grants	31.0

* Respondents rarely commented on every one of the suggested activities. The maximum number commenting on any one activity was three hundred, the minimum, one hundred.

Lest these observations create the impression that trustees of staffed foundations, unlike their counterparts in trustee-operated organizations, exercise relatively little influence on day-to-day program decisions, one should hasten to add that study data suggest the contrary. Twenty-three percent of all foundations with either full-time or part-time staff indicated the existence of a mixed trustee-staff committee. The most frequently cited activity of the committee (reported by 77 percent of the foundations with such a committee) was that of making recommendations to the full board on program matters. Sixty-five percent of these committees review and evaluate recommended projects, and 64 percent actually screen requests for grants. Other foundations (16 percent of the study's universe of 662) reported the existence of a special committee composed exclusively of trustees that exercises responsibility in the program area comparable to that of the mixed trustee-staff committee. Some 15 percent of the study's universe of foundations reported the existence of executive committees, about a third of which include operating officers among the members. An executive committee's major role (reported in 77 percent of the cases) is to operate in lieu of the board in program and other matters.[3]

It is also true that program officers or other staff members may actually make grants without the direct approval of the board. In the Ford Foundation, for example, senior program officers, with the approval of the president, may recommend grants that come within a program for which the trustees have previously made a general appropriation. A not dissimilar staff power exists on a smaller scale in other foundations, the grants being made either within the confines of a trustee-approved program or under the terms of a general appropriation made by the trustees often without designation as to program or purpose. Eighty-four foundations within the study's universe report that various members of their staff have some grant-making authority within a trustee-approved program. Five foundations report that the senior staff can make grants amounting to something less than $5,000. In eight foundations, this group can make grants of as much as $5,000, and in three foundations, $25,000 is the maximum. With the approval of the chief executive, or one or more trustees, the staff in six other foundations can make grants of less than $5,000. In seven, in which staff grants can be made under the same conditions, the ceiling is $5,000, and in three, $10,000. In some foundations, the chief executive alone can make grants of varying magnitude: less than $5,000 in six foundations, as much as $5,000 in ten others, as much as $10,000 in six others, and as much as $25,000 in four foundations.

"Staff" grants of this kind introduce a degree of flexibility into the foundation's operations that would be lacking if all such allocations had to be submitted in advance to an infrequently convened board. In addition such "retail" activities of the staff prevent cluttering up board agenda and save board time for more general and, presumably, more useful discussion.

---

[3] Other statistics developed by the study on the role of trustees suggest an even more intimate involvement of trustees in program matters and in the general management of the foundation. In these cases, however, the figures clearly embrace foundations that have no staff and are therefore actually administered by the trustees. Thus, 438 foundations report that trustees determine foundation policy; 407 state that the board ratifies or denies projects; 398 say that trustees consider projects in considerable detail; 165 say that they develop and amend projects; and 226 assert that the trustees actually originate projects.

In matters affecting finance and investment, it may be of interest to note that 125 foundations report that one trustee has been designated to look after such activities; 115 say that the trustees as a group must authorize investment changes; and 196 say that principal financial and investment matters have been delegated either to an investment counsel or to a bank or trust officer.

For additional data on trustee activity, see Appendix I.

Job Mobility in the Staffed Foundations

Wherever there is the degree of staff specialization previously described, there is usually a variety of titles for each of the functional categories of foundation personnel. These titles have therefore been classified under the following functional headings that will be used throughout the text:

——Chief executive officer
—— Deputy chief executive officer
——Communications/information officer
——Internal administrative officer
——Senior secretarial officer
——Senior financial officer
——Senior secretarial-financial officer
——Junior secretarial-financial officer
——Senior program officer
——Junior program officer
——Staff specialist

It should be reiterated that staff specialization involving all these categories is limited to a very few foundations and that, among even them, with the exception of the Ford and Rockefeller foundations, the number of individuals involved is small.

Nevertheless, as reports to the study indicated, there is sufficient job differentiation among a large enough number of foundations to make possible a rather surprising amount of movement from job to job within individual foundations. Such movement may be a promotion to a more advanced post or reassignment to a new post. Fifty-three foundations reported that, in the previous five years, they had promoted a total of 150 people. The actual statistics are given in Table 20.

Table 20. Staff Promotions Among Foundations

Number of Foundations	Number Reported Promoted from Within by Each Foundation	Total Staff Involved
33	1	33
7	2	14
7	3	21
3	4	12
2	5	10
1	60	60
Total 53		150

The existence of movement of such proportions was corroborated by the responses from individual foundation administrators, 201 of whom said they had held at least one position in their foundation of current employment prior to their existing assignment. The job held just prior to their present position had lasted for an average of 5.4 years. Ninety respondents said they had held two jobs, and thirty-eight, three jobs, prior to their present posts. The jobs held within the foundation immediately prior to the one currently held are indicated in Table 21.

Table 21. Staff Jobs Held in a Foundation Prior to Existing One

Number of Respondents	Job Title
31	Senior program officer
30	Junior program officer
23	Field representative
18	Staff specialist
17	Junior secretarial-financial officer
17	Deputy chief executive officer
16	Consultant
8	Senior secretarial officer
6	Senior financial officer
6	Internal administrative officer
3	Communications/information officer
2	Chief executive
1	Senior secretarial-financial officer
23	Other
Total 201	

In-Service Orientation and Training Programs

In a very few foundations in which a relatively high degree of staff specialization exists, in-service programs have sometimes been developed to provide training for new staff members. At least four of the better staffed foundations indicated that they have felt the need for some form of on-the-job training, although in all cases the training provided is described as "informal." Details supplied by two of these foundations reveal that programs are based on the individual's needs and interests.

Typically, an orientation program is developed after the decision has been made to add a staff member in either the program or administrative area. The new staff member spends some time with the principal officers and/or department heads of the foundation (the president, the vice president[s], the treasurer, the secretary), thus gaining familiarity with the foun-

dation's operating methods and its office policies and procedures, with emphasis on those that will affect his assignment. An hour or two, or a morning, spent in the principal administrative sections of the foundation usually suffices for this part of the orientation. If the newcomer is a program officer, part of the orientation may consist of field visits to universities involved in the foundation's program, and even of site visits to see a foundation-supported program in action, often in the company of a senior program officer on the staff. Then, for the first month or two of his employment, he is under the direct guidance of the director of the program or department, or he works in tandem with a senior colleague within the program area or department.

In one foundation, the procedure of site visits is used extensively in connection with staff being prepared for overseas service. In these cases, the total orientation program takes on a more formal or structured outline, and it may continue for as long as a month. As noted earlier in this chapter, overseas staff must frequently operate more independently than home-office staff; therefore, it is not surprising that greater attention is paid to the former's indoctrination.

New administrative staff members of another foundation make site visits of a different sort, spending periods of time with the foundation's investment counsel and with the financial officers of colleges and universities that receive support from the foundation.

In one of the country's larger foundations—one that indicated it had no formal orientation program for new staff—the new staff member traditionally spends up to his first three or four years under the wing of a more senior colleague. Although new or junior staff members attend the regular staff meetings, during this extended introductory period of employment, they have little access to the head of the foundation except as a senior colleague serves as the intermediary.

If training programs for new staff members are relatively undeveloped, programs for staff members promoted or transferred to new responsibilities are nonexistent. This is true despite evidence that, in a number of foundations, staff members are shifted from one program to another as the foundations shifts its program priorities. The transferred staff member is expected to learn on the job. No foundation provides any formal "inside" retraining or reorientation course for the employed staff member. Nor does any foundation provide any formal "outside" training or retraining. To be sure, at least seven of the managerially more advanced foundations have policies permitting either paid or unpaid leave or the payment of tuition costs for courses taken at appropriate institutions. Such courses are regarded as a contribution to staff development, but they may or may not relate directly to the work in which the staff member is engaged.

Some of the more advanced foundations also finance travel costs for staff attending professional meetings. Usually, too, these foundations allow staff members time to prepare papers in the field of their professional interest or training. In certain cases, the foundation covers the costs of professional society dues and of subscriptions to professional journals. Three foundations go a step further and specifically encourage staff members to take an active part in their professional societies by holding office in the societies or by participating in professional seminars. Such privileges are valued by the staff member and are important contributions to his overall development; but they exist in relatively few foundations and, as already suggested, are not a substitute for formal training for a foundation assignment and are not intended to be.

The Use of Consultants

As suggested earlier, the better-staffed foundations are more likely to employ consultants than are foundations with limited staff or no staff at all. Indeed, among the managerially advanced foundations, the number of consultants employed during the course of a year may sometimes be greater than the number of full-time staff. For example, the Ford Foundation reported a consultant roster that is almost twice as large as its full-time executive staff (484 consultants as against 262 full-time executive-level staff). A second foundation, one of the larger community foundations, reported a hundred consultants and a staff of five. A third reported fifty-seven consultants serving in the structure of two advisory committees to programs, and a staff of nine. Generally, of course, the consultant total is more modest. Nevertheless, only a minority of the more progressive foundations fail to include a group of consultants among those who contribute to their operations. The table below shows the distribution of paid consultants among 115 reporting foundations, classified according to origin and program (see Table 22).

Consultants may be employed full-time or part-time or on a *per diem* basis, and their tour of duty may be indefinite or of limited duration. Often, staff executives of a foundation who have retired from active duty or accepted employment elsewhere are given the status of consultants, either to cushion the economic transition to full retirement or to new employment, or to make it possible for the foundation to continue to benefit from the experience and specialized knowledge of such persons, or for both reasons. Occasionally, consultants are former staff executives, displaced by changes in the foundation's program. They continue as consultants prior to the age of retirement, with the foundation assigning them the role of elder statesmen, again partly for reasons of foundation policy and partly because the

Table 22. Number of Consultants Employed by Different Types of Foundations

Number of Consultants	Family General Purpose	Family Supportive	Family Operating	Community	Company-Sponsored	Total
1	3	33	3	2	5	46
	14.3%	51.6%	25.0%	25.0%	50.0%	40.0%
2	2	14	4	1	1	22
	9.5%	21.9%	33.3%	12.5%	10.0%	19.1%
3–5	6	9	3	1	2	21
	28.6%	14.0%	25.0%	12.5%	20.0%	18.2%
6 75	8	8	2	3	2	23
	38.1%	12.5%	16.7%	37.5%	20.0%	20.0%
75+	2	0	0	1	0	3
	9.5%	0.0%	0.0%	12.5%	0.0%	2.7%
Total	21	64	12	8	10	115
	18.3%	55.7%	10.4%	7.0%	8.6%	100.0%

foundation feels a moral obligation to continue employment for a time. In the case of the very large foundations, specialists may serve for a year or two as consultants to one of the foundation's programs prior to joining the foundation as a full-time staff member (see discussion in Chapter 3 of how people come to foundations). Normally, consultants are recruited from outside the foundation, the greater number coming from the universities, with some from business and from government as well.

Among the more sophisticated foundations, the purposes for which consultants are employed vary, although their use is usually related to program rather than to internal administration or finance. Use of consultants in the latter two areas is more prevalent among foundations with little or no staff. Program consultants may be employed to survey or resurvey a foundation's area of concern and activity and to make recommendations to staff and trustees. They may be employed to advise on the administration of a new, and possibly unusual, program for which existing permanent staff does not provide the individuals with the necessary training and background. Program consultants may also be employed to avoid expanding the permanent staff. In programs conducted outside the United States in places where it is difficult or even impossible to recruit staff locally, specialists from universities or from the professions may take on limited assignments for a foundation. Whatever these individuals may be called, they are essentially consultants as the term has been defined in this study.

In conducting certain types of program, a foundation often finds that consultants drawn from universities or from the professions are of particular value. If, for example, a foundation conducts a scholarship or fellowship program, the advice of such consultants in identifying the best and most promising talent is indispensable. Similarly, a foundation can scarcely avoid relying on consultants if it seeks to dispose of funds for highly specialized research. Staff resources of even the best-manned foundation may be inadequate to provide the guidance required if research funds are to be applied with discrimination and enjoy maximum impact.

In a somewhat broader and more philosophical sense, consultants are essential in maintaining a dialogue between a foundation and the institutional and personal recipients of its funds. On the foundation's part, the dialogue may, in some instances, amount to little more than a public relations gesture designed to maintain cordial relations with the academic and other communities. Generally, however, the dialogue should be, and usually is, of the greatest value to the responsible foundation programmer, who feels keenly the need to keep his lines open to those actively engaged in research, education, and the administration of matters with which the program is concerned. For it is chiefly in this way that the programmer keeps abreast of intellectual and social trends and makes it possible for his foundation to carry out its professed mission of supporting newly felt social needs and assisting in the community's intellectual, scientific, and artistic advance.

From what has been said above about the employment of foundation staff, it is clear that it is almost impossible to generalize. Practice varies according to the size and type of foundation, and especially according to the nature of the foundation's program. Only among the managerially advanced foundations is there a semblance of specialization as to function within the organization. Among this small group of foundations, programming responsibilities usually are separated from internal administrative duties, or there is a discernible trend in this direction, and administrative officers and program staff operate in distinctive spheres. Because of the specialized nature of the program activity, program officers and staff in this group of foundations often are much more intimately involved in designing and administering projects for which the foundation spends its money than is the case with the run-of-the-mill supportive foundation.

It is only this small minority of foundations that illustrate Amitai Etzioni's observation that the main sociological characteristic of modernization is differentiation.[4] Except for this minority, foundations bear little resemblance to the professional and semi-professional organizations of which he writes. As we have noted, most staffed foundations belong to the other

---

[4] Amitai Etzioni, *Modern Organizations*, Englewood Cliffs, New Jersey: Prentice-Hall, Inc., 1964, p. 106.

end of the staffing spectrum. They operate with a single paid executive, on a part-time or full-time basis. That executive is a "generalist" and assumes responsibility for all facets of the foundation's activity. In between this extreme and the small minority that are reasonably well staffed are those foundations, again relatively few, with from two to five persons of executive stature. Among these, there may be the beginnings of what Etzioni describes. At any rate, among them, one discerns at least the rudiments of functional specialization for administrative purposes, although rarely for program purposes.

3

Preparation, Recruitment,
and Retirement of Staff

As with other aspects of foundation personnel administration, there is a wide variety of practice relating to preparation and recruitment of candidates for service with foundations. These differences reflect the variation in the type of foundation—its asset size, the kind of program it supports, and even the degree to which it has already accepted the idea of a paid staff. Among foundation heads and personnel officers opinion also varies considerably on the personal qualities to be sought in a candidate, on the educational and professional background the candidate should possess, and on whether or not a candidate ought to undergo formal training in foundation or philanthropic administration. Similarly, when it comes to selecting the actual person for a job and persuading him to accept it, procedure varies so much that analysis and generalization are quite difficult and often impossible. Only in the matter of retirement from foundation employment is there some degree of uniformity.

Educational Backgrounds

The study's data suggest that the formal preparation of those who enter foundation service displays a variety only equalled by the diversity of their professional and occupational backgrounds. The largest number of respondents (29 percent) have a doctoral degree (Ph.D. or equivalent). The next most frequently cited degree is the baccalaureate, the highest degree of 28 percent of respondents. A master of arts degree, a master of business administration, or a master of public administration is the highest degree for just under 22 percent. Approximately 12 percent cite a law degree as their highest, and more than 6 percent of the respondents either have had no college background or have left college without taking a degree. This figure is supported by the reporting foundations, fifty-nine of which state that they employ at least one major staff person without a degree. One and one-half percent of the study's respondents are trained as doctors of medicine.

Listings of the highest degrees and fields of study of respondents, divided as to managerially advanced foundations and other foundations, appear in the following table.

Table 23. Distribution of Highest Degrees Among Staff of Managerially Advanced Foundations and of Other Foundations

Degree	Managerially Advanced Foundations	Other Foundations
Ph.D.	96 (34.5%)	24 (18.1%)
B.A.	66 (23.7%)	50 (37.7%)
M.A.	46 (16.5%)	20 (15.1%)
Law Degree	33 (11.9%)	16 (12.1%)
M.B.A., M.D., M.P.A. and other	23 (8.4%)	10 (8.0%)
None	14 (5.0%)	12 (9.0%)
Total	278 (100.0%)	132 (100.0%)

Not unexpectedly, there is a higher percentage of people in the less advanced foundations for whom the B.A. is the top degree, whereas the major foundations have almost twice the percentage of Ph.D.'s.

Among the degree-holders, as shown in Table 24, the social and behavioral sciences are the most popular fields of specialization. Other fields in order of importance are humanities, law, physical and biological sciences, and business.

In foundations of all types, there are more social and behavioral scientists than people from any other field, and these disciplines are especially well represented in the managerially advanced foundations. In the less advanced foundations, by contrast, the percentage of people with backgrounds in business studies is almost three times that of the advanced foundations.

Previous Professional Experience

The variety of professional and occupational backgrounds cited by foundation staff participating in the study may come as a surprise to

Table 24. Fields in which Respondents to Career Questionnaire Have Obtained Their Degrees

Field	Percentage Respondents
Social and behavioral sciences	41.9
Humanities	13.3
Law	12.0
Physical and biological sciences	11.6
Business administration	10.0
No field indicated	7.6
Other	3.6
Total	100.0

Table 25. Distribution of Academic Fields among Staff of Managerially Advanced and of Other Foundations

Field	Managerially Advanced Foundations Percent	Other Foundations Percent
Social and behavioral sciences	47.0	31.4
Humanities	13.0	13.9
Law	11.9	12.4
Physical and biological sciences	11.2	12.4
Business	6.7	16.8
No answer	6.7	9.5
Other	3.5	3.6
Total	100.0	100.0

some observers of the foundation scene. Few enter foundation work directly upon leaving a college or university. The actual figure probably is less than 3 percent. Of fourteen areas of previous employment identified by the study, the most popular as a stepping stone to foundation employment is, not unexpectedly, college and university teaching or administration. A total of 284 respondents have had experience in this area in either their previous, next to last, or third from last, job prior to joining their present foundation. Seven have been heads of colleges or universities. Within the overall category of college/university teaching/administration, the position of professor (any rank) was cited most frequently, followed in order of frequency by that of member of the administrative staff below a dean or general officer. In both cases, most respondents held the position just before coming to the foundation, rather than at one or two jobs removed.

Next in frequency of background is corporate manufacturing or selling. Tied for third place are service with the United States Government and with nonprofit institutions. Both areas appear to be popular launching platforms for foundation positions. In the government, the most frequently cited actual jobs are those of specialist or staff member of a government agency or institute or head or staff member of a regular government department. Foundation administrators coming from nonprofit organizations list positions as staff members or heads of institutes in the health, educational, research, and assorted other areas.

The communications industry is next in frequency in the number of people supplied foundations followed closely by banking, investment, and finance. In the case of communications, the larger number come from jobs as writers, editors, or reporters on magazines, newspapers, or press or wire services. In the broad category of banking, investment, and insurance, the position of vice president or other officer of a commercial or savings bank is cited by more respondents than any other within the category.

Prior to coming to their present positions, forty-eight foundation administrators reported they had been self-employed as businessmen or professionals. Of this group, almost half worked as lawyers. Thirty-six respondents reported experience in state, municipal, and local governments, the positions at the state level being more numerous than those at county or city levels. In some thirty instances, international agencies were mentioned as former employers of present foundation staff, and a few respondents (twenty) cited teaching or administrative positions in schools as their field of previous employment. The fine and performing arts supplied the smallest number of foundation administrators, this field having been identified by sixteen respondents, fifteen of whom had been managers or administrative staff members of organizations.

In twenty-one instances, another foundation had been the previous employer of existing foundation staff. Because mobility among foundations, that is, personnel moving from one foundation to another, is an important aspect of the larger issue of foundation service as a profession or career, an issue discussed in Chapter 6, it may be useful to examine a little more closely the statistics on those respondents listing service in another foundation as one of their three jobs prior to the one held when they responded to the study's questionnaire. The table that follows indicates the types of foundations in which the twenty-one staff members, who cited previous positions in other foundations, are currently employed and the types of foundations in which these people held their previous position. If one is to draw a conclusion from these limited data, it is that employment mobil-

Table 26. Types of Foundations in which Twenty-One Executives Held Present and Earlier Positions

	Types of Foundations in which Respondents Hold Present Jobs	Types of Foundations in which Same Group of Respondents Held Earlier Job
Family General Purpose	15	13
Family Supportive	3	3
Family Operating	2	3
Company-Sponsored	1	1
Community	——	1
Total	21	21

ity within the foundation community is largely confined to members of a small group of reasonably well-staffed, general purpose foundations.

The listing which follows shows the areas in which staff members from a selection of the managerially more sophisticated foundations and from the less advanced foundations held jobs immediately prior to coming to their present positions. As Table 27 suggests, the kind of previous professional or occupational experience foundations seek in candidates for employment varies somewhat with different types of foundations. Thus, although academic experience and government service are popular with all types of foundations, they are especially popular in the case of staff coming to the general purpose, managerially advanced foundations. Such experience is less popular with the less advanced foundations, which prefer prior service in corporate manufacturing and selling, banking, investment, and insurance. This preference is not surprising since, by definition, these foundations look for candidates who can handle both program and internal administrative duties and who are especially competent to discharge the latter. International agencies appear to be a fruitful source of candidates for the more sophisticated foundations, and self-employed business or professional persons, particularly lawyers, are good candidates for the less advanced foundations.

From the foregoing, it is apparent that candidates for a foundation appointment offer occupational or professional experiences that cover a considerable spectrum and that any of these experiences may prove of value in discharging some foundation role. This opinion is confirmed by staff respondents in their discussion of the kinds of earlier experience they find useful in their present foundation work. Inevitably, these respondents

Table 27. Areas in which Foundation Staff People Held Jobs Just Prior to Coming to Foundation Service

Area	Staffs of Managerially Advanced Foundations Percent	Staffs of Less Advanced Foundations Percent
College or university teaching or administrative staff	37.0	20.8
Nonprofit organization	12.1	13.3
United States Government	12.1	1.7
Corporate manufacturing or selling	8.7	19.2
Communications	6.8	4.2
Banking, investment, and insurance	4.9	12.5
International agencies	4.5	0.8
Other foundations	4.2	5.0
Self-employed business or profession	3.4	14.2
Other, including state or local government, school-level teaching or administration, fine and performing arts, armed forces, and miscellaneous	6.3	8.3
Total	100.0	100.0

tend to identify as useful whatever previous experience they have had, and the areas cited as useful thus closely parallel their actual experience. Hence, the relative ranking of experience according to its usefulness is about the same as relative frequency ranking in the areas of experience from which respondents came to their foundation positions.

Some variations do occur. As might perhaps be expected, in identifying *useful* experience, a larger percentage of respondents from the more advanced foundations stress such items as the value of college teaching, research, and administration; travel and other experience abroad; and employment with the United States or a foreign government. The staffs of the less advanced foundations place more emphasis on business experience, banking and investment and, in so doing, reflect both their actual professional backgrounds and the nature of their current foundation jobs.

Opinions on Training for Foundation Service

In the course of the study, an attempt was made to ascertain the opinions of the foundation world on what might be done to train persons directly for philanthropic administration, either before entering into the service or

Table 28. Previous Professional Experience of Most Use in a Foundation

	Staffs of Managerially Advanced Foundations Percent	Staffs of Other Foundations Percent
College or university administration	20.0	17.0
College or university teaching or research	20.0	4.4
Service with United States or foreign government	19.0	4.4
Banking, investment, or insurance	13.7	24.0
Travel, observations, or experience abroad, whether employed or unemployed	11.6	2.2
Experience related to foundation's needs and interests	11.0	9.5
General business experience	9.8	15.3
Research or demonstration project	8.4	5.0
Previous foundation experience	6.3	4.4
The armed forces	4.6	5.1
The United Nations, a specialized agency, or a private international group	3.2	—
Voluntary activity in community affairs	2.8	0.5
Independent profession other than law	2.5	3.6
Law	2.1*	3.6*
Ad hoc public or private body	2.0	2.2
Other, including serving as consultant to a nonprofit organization, special contact with intellectual leaders, academic administration below college level, fund raising, management consulting, social agency or health service, teaching at elementary or secondary level, service as trustee of a nonprofit organization, service in a public funding agency such as NIH or NSF	9.3	16.8
Total	146.3**	118.0**

* It may be of some interest to note that the percentage of respondents who reported having law degrees is much higher than the percentage of lawyers who said they found this discipline useful in their present foundation position.
** Responses total more than 100 percent because respondents cited more than one item.

immediately after appointment. Although a sizable group of respondents reacted positively to suggested methods of training people for foundation service, there was little agreement as to the way in which preparation might be implemented.

As indicated in the table which follows (Table 29), internship programs within the foundation community are by far the most popular of three suggested modes of training, and these programs also rank high in the ideas volunteered by respondents.[1] The suggestion of formal courses in foundation administration at the university level received support from only 20 percent of respondents. This suggestion also garnered the greatest number of opposing votes. In general comments made on the subject, the most frequent (13 percent of respondents) was that such courses are definitely *not* a desirable way in which to prepare for foundation service. Under 2 percent of the respondents commented on the possible usefulness of having existing university courses in administration incorporate more material

Table 29. Opinions of Staff People on Education and Training for Foundation Service

1. *Responses to Suggestions Made in Questionnaire:*	*Yes*	*No*	*No Response*
Internship programs within the foundation community	68.2%	18.7%	13.1%
More information available in schools about foundations	39.1%	41.0%	19.9%
Formal courses in foundation administration at the university level	20.1%	67.1%	12.8%
2. *Suggestions Initiated by Respondents:*		*Mentioned*	
Formal courses in foundation administration at university level *not* desirable		13.0%	
Internship and in-service courses		9.2%	
Expertness in foundation's areas of interest		8.8%	
Good liberal arts background		5.7%	
Formal courses in foundation administration at university level		3.8%	
Summer workshops for foundation personnel		1.9%	
More attention to subject of managing nonprofit organizations in existing university courses		1.7%	

---

[1] Nevertheless, as noted earlier in Chapter 2, few foundations have given any serious thought to internship programs.

on the management of nonprofit institutions, and specifically on the administration of foundations.

A few of the more articulate supporters of specialized training for foundation service pointed out that both grantors and grantees are occasionally inefficient in managing money and that, consequently, foundations ought to insist on improving their fiscal and accounting practices as well as their program operations. It is particularly desirable, say these few critics, for programmers to acquire some knowledge of balance sheets and similar mundane matters if they are to improve their record in monitoring and appraising projects.

Some respondents expressed the opinion that specialized preparation in administration would be helpful to the smaller and medium-sized foundations that might be planning to take their first step in acquiring staff. Still others insisted that all foundations could well afford to upgrade personnel and that some kind of formal instruction on managerial principles, sound fiscal practices, and the role of private philanthropy was precisely the prescription that would-be, and even existing, foundation administrators need.

Regarding opinions among different types of foundations, 36 percent of those employed by the less advanced foundations favor formal courses in foundation administration, while only 12 percent of their counterparts in the managerially advanced foundations share this view. Thus, it is the generalists who appear to be most favorably disposed toward some kind of formal training. Behind this seeming anomaly is the fact that it is these generalists in the less advanced foundations who are faced with the broadest span of operating decisions in foundation administration. The staffs of the greater foundations, by contrast, are called upon to perform more specialized tasks, for which their previous education and even their professional experience have prepared them. Therefore, as far as this latter group is concerned, formal training in foundation administration *per se* would be of less use.

Perhaps one reason for the relative lack of interest in formal preparation is the emphasis that foundation people are wont to place on certain attributes of mind and personality, often rating them higher than knowledge or administrative skill. One of these attributes, repeatedly mentioned by respondents, and rated above all others, is "soundness of judgment," presumably the ability to weigh various, and often conflicting, aspects of some matter and then make the "right" decision. It is a tenuous quality, partly innate, partly the result of practical experience, a quality in demand in many quarters and obviously appealing to appointing officers of foundations.

"Ability to maintain good relations with trustees and others" ranks second among the attributes sought while "administrative ability," "general knowledge" and "ability to present ideas orally and in writing," rank respectively third, fourth, and fifth in the rating scale. "Depth or extent of knowledge of professional field" significantly ranked last and was less than half as popular among respondents as "soundness of judgment." The following table lists the percentages of foundation heads agreeing on the relative importance of each of these various attributes.

Table 30. Qualities that Foundation Heads Consider Desirable in a Good Foundation Administrator*

Quality	Percent who agree**
Soundness of judgment	77.3
Ability to maintain good relations with trustees and others	62.0
Administrative ability	60.4
General knowledge	57.9
Ability to present ideas orally and in writing	48.0
Imagination and creative capacity	47.5
Ability to coordinate efforts of others	44.0
Commitment to social improvement	42.2
Depth or extent of knowledge of professional field	35.2

* The number of responses on which this question is based is 242.
** The authors have defined "agreement" as the percentage of respondents who indicate a rating of 4 or 5 on a scale of 0–5.

The fact that the less tangible qualities are often more highly prized than general or specialized knowledge, and the relative indifference to formal preparation and training for foundation service suggest that the tradition of the able and adaptable amateur—the generalist—symbolized by the careers of men like Flexner and Rose, still has considerable viability. That the amateur tradition does indeed continue to enjoy acceptance is reiterated in the testimony of one of the most distinguished contemporary foundation administrators. In a letter to the study's directors he asserted that the best men in the field seem to have little in common. Some, he said, are knowledgeable in their professional field; others, equally successful, have only a superficial grasp. Moreover, few foundation officers with whom he had come in contact during his career had much administrative ability in the conventional sense, but they all had qualities that made one admire them very much. These qualities always seemed to succeed in making one overlook the sometimes equally obvious defects. This observer concluded his remarks with the statement that successful foundation officials and staff people are probably born, not made.

Some Evidence of an Opposing Trend

The continued popularity of the amateur tradition must not, however, be allowed to obscure the fact that a different view also exists. Although staff members of the more sophisticated, project-oriented foundations also value the subjective qualities deemed essential for a good foundation administrator, there is evidence that people from these foundations tend to be somewhat firmer about the need for expert knowledge of a specific field that is often required to initiate, design, evaluate, and even direct projects and programs of the foundation. As the following listing indicates (Table 31), staff members from the more advanced foundations gave slightly more emphasis to the need for specialization than did their counterparts from the less advanced foundations.

Table 31. Order of Importance of Qualities that Make a Good Foundation Administrator Given by Staff Members of Managerially Advanced Foundations and by Those from Other Foundations

Qualities Sought	Ratings by Staff Members from Managerially Advanced Foundations	Ratings by Staff Members from Other Foundations
Soundness of judgment	1 (highest)	1
Ability to present ideas orally and in writing	2	5
General knowledge	3	2
Depth or extent of knowledge of professional field	4	8
Administrative ability	5	3
Commitment to social improvement	6	7
Ability to coordinate efforts of others	7	6
Ability to maintain good relations with trustees and others outside foundation	8 (lowest)	4

This preference for specialists is underscored by the action of some of the leading foundations in acquiring staff for program purposes. Thus, one foundation that plans to enter the field of molecular biology has sought as its program specialist an organic chemist or physiological psychologist, or at least someone with training in a peripheral discipline. A second foundation, planning a fellowship project in the physical sciences, secured a distinguished organic chemist. A third foundation, planning to support mathematics, went looking for a mathematician. Still another, proposing to go into the field of engineering, looked for and secured the services of a seasoned civil engineer.

Additional examples of a possible drift toward specialization are implied by recent personnel developments at the Ford Foundation. In 1967, Ford announced the appointment of a new vice president for national affairs to be concerned chiefly with urban matters. His background was identified as "six years of strenuous service in New Haven and New York on the front lines of the urban crisis." In the same year, the foundation appointed a programmer to train potential leaders for developing countries and described his background as six years of service as the "linchpin of the African Bureau of the Department of State." A year earlier, the foundation had announced that, as a result of some administrative restructuring, it had been "able to give a new freedom of action to several of its senior officers . . . matching their specific assignments to their experience and current interests" (see the annual reports of the Ford Foundation for the years mentioned).

These actions suggest that the recommendation on personnel of the Gaither Committee, which strongly supported the amateur tradition, may have been pushed rather far back on the shelf at the Ford Foundation. Indeed, examples of hiring specialized personnel proliferate among the major foundations and those examples are by no means restricted to the past few years. The growing incidence of this practice among leading foundations may, therefore, forecast a gradual shift away from the gifted generalist, still favored by the majority of foundations, toward the acquisition of staff with training and experience that are relevant to particular positions. Such a shift could eventually cause leading foundations to reexamine their existing indifferent attitude toward formal training for foundation administrative posts.

Recruiting Foundation Staff

Given the nature of the foundation world's attitude toward the education and background of those currently employed, it is, perhaps, in character that the process of discovering and hiring personnel should be as informal and unstructured as was intimated at the beginning of this chapter.

According to evidence submitted to the study's directors, the majority of foundation administrators find their jobs as a result of the recommendation of a staff or board member of the employing foundation. More than 40 percent of all appointments result from such a direct recommendation.

The second most favored route to a foundation position is appointment following a recommendation by a third party. The recommending third party may, of course, be any one of a number of people, and he may or may not be a person of considerable experience, well acquainted with the capabilities of the person recommended. The employment broker may be a university professor who recommends a former or, occasionally, current student. Or he may be the foundation's attorney or investment counselor, or possibly the auditor. Sometimes brokers of this sort, or their firms, recommend associates, or even partners, who are not likely to make the grade in their own firm. Sometimes, when they are thus recommended to a foundation, they do not make the grade in the foundation either. Nor would recommendation by a golfing companion of a trustee or chief executive be without precedent. Occasionally, too, like John Alden, the third party broker forgets his Myles Standish and becomes so enamoured of the prospective foundation position that he supplements the plea for his protégé with a plea for himself—and gets the job. One respondent conceded quite frankly that, "I was asked to find someone to be a candidate for the job. In time, I convinced myself I had the qualifications."

Major, project-oriented foundations that may be in the market for specialized personnel to staff an internal "action" program or an unusual grants program often try to find their people by making discreet inquiries in the scholarly or professional worlds. In this case, the third party brokers are likely to be faculty or professional colleagues of those chosen. In other cases, those chosen may have headed some research operation that the foundation had funded.

Respondents noted instances of employment being secured through direct personal application, certainly not one of the effective routes, although 3 percent more respondents from the managerially advanced foundations cited it than did those from the lesser foundations. One leading foundation has recruited some of its top executives in this manner. In the past decade, it has accepted several applicants for junior positions, and among these, two or three have risen quickly to the top in the foundation's hierarchy. The policy (and fact) of mobility within the organization was, of course, a factor making this kind of recruitment a success. The foundation made the original appointment to the lowest rung of the executive ladder. Subsequently, it either discouraged the young appointee's hopes for continued employed or encouraged him by promoting him.

Although the precise details of how particular individuals came to a foundation fit into one or more of the generalizations used in Table 32, the actual details of the process run the gamut from the "hero's" reward in a Horatio Alger tale to a foundation's desire to avoid the charge of racial discrimination. Actual descriptions given by respondents include: "Was officer of a bank that created the testamentary foundation" (a trust); "Was attorney for the founder"; "Got the job because I was a Jew and the foundation had never before had a Jew for an officer"; "Came up through stenog-

Table 32. Routes to Foundation Jobs

Route	Percent Citing
Recommendation of a member of the foundation staff or board	42.2
Recommendation of third party known to staff or board	26.1
Participation in a project financed by the foundation	9.7
Foundation's favorable response to a personal application	9.2
Relationship or friendship with donor or donor's family	6.6
Employment in donor's business	5.7
Foundation's inquiries at universities	4.0
Other routes, including foundation's inquiries at an executive placement center or management consulting firm, service as a trustee of the foundation, identification as having special professional competence related to foundation's need, and recommendation by another foundation	8.6
Total	112.1*

* Total is over 100% because some respondents cited more than one route.

rapher-secretarial-administrative route" (this answer was found in the case of many of the women staff members). And a last one uses one word to describe how he got the job: "nepotism."

A comparison of the methods of entry into foundation service by staffs of the thirty-five managerially advanced foundations and the less advanced foundations shows considerable differences in the case of four methods of entry. Other methods of entry seem equally popular with both types of foundations.

None of the variations in the table needs cause surprise. The managerially advanced foundations are obviously more likely to have someone

Table 33. Four Popular Routes to Foundation Jobs

Route	35 Advanced Foundations Percent	Other Foundations Percent
Recommendation of a member of the foundation staff or board	48.8	28.5
Participation in a project financed by the foundation	11.2	6.6
Employment in donor's business	2.1	13.1
Relationship or friendship with donor or donor's family	1.8	16.8

on the existing staff make recommendations on hiring future staff. Equally obviously, the less advanced organizations normally have no staff members to scout out possibilities. They may have no staff at all. Moreover, the less advanced group is more apt to give funds to existing organizations than to special projects, the latter being a more usual source of personnel for the more advanced foundations. The higher rating of family relationship or friendship for securing people in the less advanced foundations reflects a fairly well-traveled route of successful candidates to small family foundations, and the higher rating given "employment in the donor's business" reflects the sizable number of company employees who have become involved with company-sponsored foundations. Indeed, in almost all foundations created by a business enterprise or a bank, any part-time or full-time officer is likely to have come into the foundation from the sponsoring business or bank of which he previously has been an officer, and of which he may, in fact, continue to be an officer while he serves the foundation.

In commenting at some length on the subject of recruitment, one respondent to the study's questionnaire seemed to feel that the process was somewhat more systematic than the description just given. At any rate, he volunteered the view that identifying people for employment on the part of a foundation was like finding presidents and deans of colleges and universities. "A small group of established, long-term professionals are asked to suggest candidates, and these, in turn, are checked out with persons of proven wisdom as to especial competence. Probably less than one hundred persons make recommendations for virtually all the vacancies occurring within the first five hundred largest foundations." It is possible that some of the well-staffed foundations may resort to a procedure similar to the one he describes and that, occasionally, other foundations, seeking staff for the first time, may also resort to it.

On the other hand, the respondent's numbers seem to be on the generous side, both as respects the number of "professionals" who might make recommendations and the number of foundations that might be seeking staff at any one time. In any case, as the testimony of other respondents has indicated, the world of foundations is too unorganized to tolerate even this informal, albeit relatively centralized, placement agency.

Inevitably, some observers of the foundation scene and a few respondents to the study's questionnaire expressed dissatisfaction with the unsystematic way in which foundations discover staff. One such critic, a staff member of a foundation, describing his earlier attempts to obtain a foundation position, wrote: "A little over a year ago, I took a hard look at the foundation field in general and attempted to draw on some specific information on the training and employment of foundation administrators . . . This effort was a study in frustration. In fact, the advice of several leading foundation administrators seemed to indicate quite clearly that the best way to get into foundation work was to do something else."

Other critics have been especially concerned with the difficulties that stand in the way of anyone who, lacking a sponsor, may have to apply directly for a foundation position if he wishes to be considered. Obstacles to placement such as this one loom especially large for young people, many of whom, having a high sense of social commitment, feel they can fulfill that commitment by serving a foundation. To overcome these obstacles the suggestion was made by some respondents that there be established a kind of reference and clearing agency in which persons hoping to be considered for foundation employment might learn more about it and file their credentials.

It seems unlikely, however, that such a procedure will be developed—at least not in a formal sense. Not only are there various administrative hurdles to be overcome, but there are also those who look askance at the whole idea. The latter group reminds us that the total number of people to be accommodated in foundation service is severely limited and that it is not likely to climb significantly during the next decade or two. As long as the intake is thus restricted, they argue, there is no need for more systematic ways of recruiting candidates for foundation positions. What is more, since the absorption rate of candidates to jobs is so low, resorting to procedures of the overt type to encourage people—and especially young people—to apply is likely to cause disappointment and disillusionment, and perhaps even to bring discredit upon foundation service.

The Issue of Professionalism

The resolution of issues such as the foregoing, and all those raised earlier concerning preparation and recruitment, depends in large measure on whether or not foundation service should be regarded as a profession or can be regarded as a profession. To put the question in other terms, is foundation service, like law or medicine, sufficiently distinct in the knowledge and skills it requires that one can formally prepare for it? Then, having entered into it, are there, or can there be, material and intellectual rewards comparable to those of an established profession or occupation?

Opinion on this basic issue of foundation professionalism is divided. Those of the study's respondents who commented on the issue tended to support a negative point of view. One respondent writes that "to professionalize philanthropy would be a 'grievous error.' The strength of a private foundation is its individuality, its plurality, its *lack of professionalism* [his italics]. Let us not turn into morticians with annual meetings, trade associations, etc." A second respondent, reinvoking the tradition of amateurism, asserts that foundation administrators do not need unique skills:

"The desire for professionalism by hairdressers is understandable, not so with foundation administrators." And still a third declares, "I have difficulty with the whole idea of foundation work as a career. Foundations deal essentially with ideas, unlike, say, industry, which deals with products and services. You can keep on learning about your company's products and services and become progressively more valuable to it—hence you can have a career in industry. You don't necessarily get better ideas the longer you stay with a foundation. On the contrary, it has been my experience that people with the best ideas are likely to be those who come to a foundation fresh from another field. . . ."

On the other hand, a distinguished former executive of a major foundation, a man who has now returned to the university world, has taken exactly the opposite point of view. He was most emphatic in his belief that "foundation administration is emerging—and should emerge—as a distinctive profession for which the only valid training is apprenticeship."

On balance, those who resist the idea of foundation service as a profession probably have the better of the argument. At any rate, numbers are on their side. Those specifically opposed to professionalizing foundation service are augmented by others who reaffirm the amateur tradition in such service. Still others, as we have noted, invoke the amateur tradition of foundation service by insisting that certain subjective personal qualities are more important than formal learning, whether that be of a general or specialized nature. Even the apparent favor shown by some foundations for program specialists, also noted earlier, is not necessarily favorable to foundation professionalism. The "professionalism" sought in this instance is not in foundation philanthropy or administration but in a particular discipline substantively related to a foundation's program. In time this favor for training in particular disciplines may place a higher value on foundation administration *per se*, but at the moment there is no discernible connection between one and the other.

It is probable, therefore, that for the next decade or two, preparation and recruitment for foundation service will remain as unsystematic and unstructured as they are now. Although this conclusion will probably win an affirmative nod from the anti-professionalists, there are nevertheless certain liabilities. The opposition to formal preparation and the concomitant absence of any formal means of entering the service may well cut foundations off from any systematic contact with the oncoming generation who are inclined to be anti-establishment and who spawn new ideas. Even though foundation service may not offer a professional career, incumbents seem to have an affinity for generous tenure and continue in service indefinitely. This conclusion is documented by the study's data, which indicate that the average age of the administrator in the more advanced foundations is forty-eight and in the rest of the foundation community, fifty-two. Such persistence in service necessarily limits opportunities for those who would replace incumbents.

Staff Turnover and Retirement Practices

Some alleviation of this condition can, of course, be expected from normal turnover of personnel and the usual movement in and out of foundations. Further alleviation can be achieved by appropriate retirement policies.

As for turnover, comments made earlier (see Chapter 2) suggest that, especially among the better staffed foundations, personnel changes resulting from promotion, reassignment of roles, and departures from the foundation field are fairly frequent. One hundred and nine foundations taking part in the study indicated that 299 staff people had left their employment during the preceding four years. This figure is a sizable 21 percent of the employed foundation universe. Although in some cases the reason for leaving was retirement, in most cases, the executive returned to his original discipline or profession or entered a new vocation for which his foundation experience had helped to prepare him. At the same time, 136 foundations reported bringing at least one executive staff member (a total of 289 individuals) in from outside the foundation field during the preceding five years.

But a more sustained movement in and out of foundations depends principally on the establishment of a systematic retirement policy. Here, too, probably more has been done than the foundation community realizes, although the practices governing termination of an executive staff member's employment are still relatively unstructured. Of the 422 foundations from which data were sought on the question of a mandatory retirement age, 83 percent (348 foundations) indicated they had no formal retirement policy while 17 percent (74 foundations) stated they had such a policy.

Of the foundations that do have a formal policy, 74 percent indicated that the mandatory age for male executives is sixty-five, which is also the age cited for women again by 74 percent. The mandatory retirement age range for males is a wide one, with a low of sixty years in two cases and a high of seventy-five years in one. There is a similarly wide range for women executives, from fifty-five years to seventy-two. Among reporting foundations with no formal retirement policy, thirty-eight stated there is a customary age at which executives leave the organization. In this case, too, the most often cited age is sixty-five for both men and women. To sum up, of the 212 foundations which the study has ascertained employ full-time staff, slightly over half (112, or 53 percent) have either a formalized policy or a customary practice regarding retirement of executive staff. The age ranges appear in the following table which, of course, includes only those foundations that provided data on age ranges.

Table 34. Mandatory and Customary Retirement Ages for Male and Female Executives

	Under 65	*65*	*Over 65*
Mandatory age for men	3	55	11
Mandatory age for women	4	55	7
Customary age for men	1	29	2
Customary age for women	4	25	——

Staff Tenure and Changing Social Needs

To some observers the normal turnover rate of personnel in foundations, insured by existing retirement policies, does not seem adequate for keeping foundations in tune with the needs of a rapidly changing society. Concern on this score is fortified by the rather high average age level of incumbent administrators which, as was noted in a preceding paragraph, is forty-eight in the more advanced foundations and fifty-two in other foundations. The foundation community has itself exhibited its concern with this condition by the position it has taken toward the oft-suggested proposal that foundation people should enjoy somewhat the same tenure guarantees as are enjoyed by professors in most universities. On that issue there is no ambiguity: the opposition to guaranteed tenure is overwhelming.[2]

Individual respondents desirous of a more affirmative approach to this problem have suggested that greater efforts be made to bring new people, and especially young people, into the foundation fold for a limited period or on a temporary basis, thus avoiding some of the difficulties attending recruitment of young people, mentioned earlier. One respondent made the rather radical suggestion that the tenure of all but the most senior officials be limited to a term of years, possibly not more than five years, and that younger people be brought into a foundation for a term of service with the clear understanding that their ultimate career objectives lay outside the foundation fold. Others suggested an in-and-out type of service—mature scholars serving for a term of years and then returning to their original posts.

Ideas and attitudes such as these may be considered, at least impliedly, as a reiteration of the views opposed to attempts to professionalize foundation service that were canvassed on an earlier page. The immediate concern at this point, however, is to avoid aggravating an existing tendency toward lengthy tenure in foundations and, by discovering constructive ways of

---

[2] The tenure suggestion received an average rating of only 1.096 on a scale of 0 to 5. The actual ratings were: 0–181; 1–32; 2–34; 3–34; 4–19; and 5–13. See further comment in Chapter 6.

introducing new blood into the foundation cadres, to mitigate the danger that foundations will fail to keep abreast of the social needs which they should seek to satisfy.

Some of the more progressive foundations, those especially alert to the requirements of their institutional obligations and desirous of being kept aware of each new generation's priorities and views of the future, might well consider some sort of temporary internship program for younger scholars. Thus a relatively brief period of service might take place either prior to establishing more permanent affiliations in the academic and professional worlds or shortly after having been inducted into those worlds. How such a period of service could be undertaken without diverting the internees from research and other scholarly activity upon which they may already have embarked, and without injuring such activity, could pose a problem. The difficulty might be overcome, at least in part, by combining pre- and postdoctoral fellowships or internships with a sabbatical leave program for younger scholars who already have non-tenure appointments in universities or have already embarked on the first rung of the professional ladder, either in academe or elsewhere.

Foundations interested in attacking this problem of maintaining constant contact with the scholars and thinkers of each new generation might find useful suggestions in the policy recently established by Russell Sage Foundation. By means of fellowships for the graduate or immediate postgraduate student, a visiting scholar program, and interim staff appointments, this foundation assures itself of a constant and changing flow of some of the nation's best talent in its fields of interest. Both its internal program of research and its grants to outside institutions and scholars benefit from this staffing policy. Guest scholars and temporary staff people are informally integrated into the administration of the foundation and its social structure so that there is a constant interchange of ideas and advice. Both the internal and external programs of the foundation profit accordingly.

Other foundations attack the problem of recruiting new talent in indirect ways by offering fellowships to promising young scholars and artists all over the world (a policy of the John Simon Guggenheim Memorial Foundation), or by organizing research groups that use younger talent, as in the case of the Twentieth Century Fund, or by funneling research and fellowship grants to competent younger scholars, through organizations like the Social Science Research Council and similar groups. All these ways of maintaining contact with, and encouraging, new and promising talent ought to be carefully reexamined by the foundation world, especially if it persists in applying traditional ways of seeking its own immediate staff and in maintaining existing employment policies.

4

The Compensation Practices
of Foundations:
Chief Executives

No aspect of this study has inspired more questions and expressions of interest than the subject of salaries and such allied compensation as fringe benefits. Judging from the formal and informal inquiries from people within the foundation community and from others outside it, there is a keen desire for information on salaries for immediate use in specific situations. As indicated in Chapter 3, for the past four or five years there has been a moderate turnover in foundation employees, and a modest number of people are being hired from time to time. Moreover, although the fact is difficult to document, it appears that a small number of foundations are currently creating positions and contemplating additions to their staff. These activities may explain, in part, the pressing interest in foundation compensation.

A more important reason for the interest in, and demand for, data on compensation is that the foundation community lacks norms on which to base long-term compensation policies and on which to establish salary and income levels for its employees. That such should be the case ought not to occasion any surprise. The reasons for the lack of compensation norms are not difficult to discern. Their absence is explained in part by the relative isolation in which the foundation administrator operates. As pointed out earlier, unlike physicians, lawyers, or college professors, foundation administrators do not form a distinct profession. Hence, to a degree, they lack the benefits of professional integration and association including, among others, the benefit of standardization as to duties and income that professional organizations tend to establish. Moreover, people are hired by a foundation to meet a specific need, and the actual service rendered by the administrator differs considerably from one type of foundation to another. Hence, the foundations themselves have difficulty in arriving at any comparable standards for compensating their employees.

The lack of norms quickly becomes apparent in an examination of salaries for different positions in various types of foundations.[1] Looking first at the salaries of chief executives of foundations, their most obvious characteristic is their wide range. For example, full-time chief executives of family general purpose foundations earn anywhere from $25,000 to $75,000. For full-time chief executives of foundations of this type with over $100 million in assets, the average is $57,250. For full-time chief executives—on whom the study has data—who head foundations with assets below $100 million, the average is $44,300. As respects the salaries of the executives of the family general purpose foundations, the figures appear in Table 35.[2]

Since a good percentage of chief executives and other foundation staff are employed only part-time, for purposes of reporting on salary, individuals have been placed in five categories: full-time, 66–99 percent of time, 33–65 percent of time, under 33 percent of time, and time not mentioned and therefore unknown.

It is in these foundations that one would expect to find the highest

Table 35. Average Salaries of Full-Time and Part-Time Chief Executives of Family General Purpose Foundations

Percentage of time devoted to foundation	Asset Level of Foundation	
	$100 million and over	Under $100 million
100	$57,250 (Range: 75,000–40,000)	$44,300 (Range: 72,000–25,000)
66–99	60,000	32,500*
33–65	30,000	12,500
Under 33	——	15,500

* The average salaries for part-time staff members are based on time actually spent in service to the foundation and not on 100 percent of the staff members' time.

[1] Continuing the typology established earlier, foundations are divided into the following categories based on origin and program: family general purpose, family supportive, family operating, community, and company-sponsored.

[2] Because of the occasional substantial variations in salaries within individual categories of executives, the resulting averages in the tables in this and the subsequent chapter may be less meaningful than the tables in Appendix II in which averages are computed on the basis of a more detailed breakdown of foundations by asset size.

level of salaries, for these are foundations that, by definition, have more than a handful of staff who have major responsibility for program development. They are also foundations that, for the most part, have generous resources. Thus, on the basis both of ability to pay and of the qualifications, training, and responsibility of the executives, the highest salaries in the foundation community should go to chief executives of family general purpose foundations.

Among the family foundations with largely supportive programs, the largest category of foundations in the study, levels of salary are lower, and there is considerably greater use of part-time executives. From the tabula-

Table 36. Average Salaries of Full-Time and Part-Time Chief Executives of Family Supportive Foundations

Percentage of time devoted to foundation	Asset Level of Foundation	
	$100 million and over	*Under $100 million*
100	$27,333 (Range: 34,100–15,000) (F = 15,000)*	$22,691 (Range: 60,000–1,700) (F = 18,090)
66–99	$28,000	$23,350 (Range: 60,000–6,000) (F = 16,000)
33–65	37,000	15,588 (Range: 50,000–4,800) (F = 7,500)
Under 33	——	6,686 (Range: 16,000–900) (F = 5,500)
Unknown	——	13,633 (Range: 40,000–1,200)

* F = female. Wherever information is available, average salaries of female incumbents are shown separately.

tion, it is evident that for this type of foundation, there is only a very rough correlation between the size of its assets and its level of salaries for chief executives. Here, as elsewhere, there are cases of inverse correlation between the percentage of time devoted to the foundation and the level of salary. A part-time executive may receive just as much or more compensation than his full-time counterpart. This is the case, for example, among foundations with under $100 million in assets, in which the average salary for full-time chief executives is $22,691, while that for chief executives working between 65 and 99 percent of the time is $23,350. It is possible that in some family supportive foundations, individuals identified as part-time employees of the foundation also have other responsibilities related to the foundation's activity and that the foundation salary may cover both. In any case, it is well to bear in mind that the small number of individuals in some foundation categories on whom data have been collected makes generalizations hazardous at best.

Although the preponderance of family supportive foundations in the study's universe results in more data on salaries paid to executives of this type of foundation, some comparison may be made with the smaller number of reported salaries paid by family general purpose foundations. Given equality in asset size between the two types of foundations, the general purpose foundations clearly reward their executives at a higher level, substantiating the statement made earlier that the relatively high executive salaries of general purpose foundations are related both to asset size and to the duties that chief executives of these foundations are called upon to perform.

Among the chief executives of the family supportive foundations, there are eighteen women. As already noted, their salaries are shown separately in this and in subsequent tables, in order to determine whether or not any broad difference in compensation between men and women exists in the foundation community, and if so, how significant this difference may be. In the case of chief executives of family supportive foundations, the number of women chief executives increases in the lower asset ranges of foundations. In two cases, women receive the lowest salary within an asset range; in no case is a woman paid the top salary in any of the classifications established according to assets of the foundation and time spent by the chief executive on the job.

In family operating foundations, there is again a wide range of salaries for the chief executive's job, with levels lower than those of general purpose foundations, but slightly higher than those of supportive foundations with assets under $100 million. If one applies the principle that people with

Table 37. Average Salaries of Full-Time and Part-Time Chief Executives of Family Operating Foundations*

Percentage of time devoted to foundation	
100	$25,427 (Range: 45,000–4,600) (F = 17,300)
66–99	13,000
33–65	12,000

* In presenting data on the salaries of chief executives of family operating, community, and company-sponsored foundations, the relatively smaller number of salaries reported to the study have led the study's directors to omit reference to asset size of foundation.

greater responsibilities should receive compensation commensurate with those responsibilities, it would appear that the salary level for operating foundation heads is probably appropriate. A head of an operating foundation may be responsible for the management of anything from a nursing school to a research center or museum, a responsibility that seems more demanding than that of a manager of a supportive foundation who makes grants to other institutions, although probably no more demanding than what is asked of the head of a major general purpose foundation.

Salaries and salary ranges for chief executives of community and company sponsored foundations are given in the following table. Commu-

Table 38. Average Salaries of Full-Time and Part-Time Chief Executives in Community and Company-Sponsored Foundations

Percentage of time devoted to foundation	Type of Foundation	
	Community	Company-sponsored
100	$18,541	$24,000
	(Range: 40,000–3,600)	(Range: 55,000–8,000)
66–99	19,400	29,800
	(Range: 34,000–4,200)	(Range: 40,000–17,000)
33–65	8,716	6,000
	(Range: 18,000–2,400)	
Under 33	4,600	—
	(Range: 10,000–800)	
Unknown	2,400	—

nity foundations employ relatively few women chief executives and these foundations are partial to part-time employees. Data from company-sponsored foundations were more difficult to obtain than was salary information from the other types of foundations because in most company-sponsored foundations, the foundation executive's salary is paid by the founding company, and therefore not reported as an administrative expense of the foundation. As in the case of the family supportive foundations and the community foundations, some part-time chief executives of company-sponsored foundations seem to be compensated at a higher rate than are full-time executives.

The Seniority Factor in the Compensation of Full-Time Chief Executives

Because there are more data on the salaries of chief executives than on any other category of foundation staff member—due in part to the fact that many foundations have only a chief executive officer—it is perhaps worthwhile to examine their salary levels from other points of view. The first might be the length of time on the job. To what extent, if any, is level of compensation of chief executives related to the number of years an incumbent has held his or her present job? The following relationships emerge.

Table 39. Average Salaries of Full-Time Chief Executives with Tenure of Five Years or Less and with Tenure of More than Five Years

Type of Foundation	Five Years or Less	More than Five Years
Family General Purpose	$50,450	$44,812
Family Supportive	25,451	24,821
Family Operating	27,062	29,800
Community	16,157	19,075
Company-Sponsored	39,500	17,800

From this brief tabulation it might appear that salaries increase slightly in family operating and community foundations as the length of service of the incumbent job holder increases. On the other hand, for the family general purpose, family supportive, and company-sponsored foundations, increased years of service appear to go unrewarded, at least relatively, since the salary level of those with less than five years of service is more than the level of those with more than five years of service. Doubtless what has happened is that chief executives hired within the last five years have commanded starting salaries higher even than the existing salaries of incumbents who have been running a foundation in these categories for longer than five years. The effects of inflation, the increase in academic compensation, and even, perhaps, the more recently felt need for better, and hence more costly, talent may all have contributed to this disparity in salary levels as a result of which the more recently appointed appear to be favored as against those who have been in service for some time.

Salary Levels in Different Regions of the Country

Again, focusing on the chief executives, incumbents in the different types and sizes of foundations have been classified along geographic lines in order to ascertain whether salary levels vary from one part of the country to another. In the ensuing tabulation, the same geographical divisions are used as were used in the discussion of the geographical distribution of administrators in Chapter 1.

To anyone familiar with comparative salaries in other fields, it should come as no surprise that salaries for foundation chief executives in the

Table 40. Average Salaries of Full-Time Chief Executives in Five Regions of the United States*

Type of Foundation	Northeast	New York City**	Southeast	North Central	South Central	West
Family General Purpose	$54,678	$54,678	$35,000	$39,680	$ ——	$ ——
Family Supportive	25,243	27,095	24,725	19,555	18,972	20,942
Family Operating	28,455	32,366	38,500	27,375	10,100	16,700
Community	18,525	30,000	5,500	20,000	——	17,500
Company-Sponsored	32,700	16,100	——	22,225	8,000	——

* For the breakdown of states included in each region see Figure I.

** Although the figures for New York City are included in the figures for the Northeast, they are shown separately because of the heavy concentration of foundation wealth and activity in New York City.

81

Northeast, led by salaries in New York City, are, for the most part, higher than those in other parts of the country. With the exception of community foundations and a single case of a chief executive of a family operating foundation in the Southeast, chief executives are better paid in the Northeast than in other regions of the country. In family general purpose foundations, salaries in the Northeastern states considerably exceed those in all other regions. In family supportive foundations, chief executives in the Southeast region earn almost as much as those in the Northeast, and the same is true for foundation heads of family operating foundations in the North Central region in comparison with those in the Northeast.

Recent Trends and Comparisons

Records of salaries of foundation executives made public by the Internal Revenue Service in the last three or four years show that in this period, many chief executive officers have received major salary increases. For example, examination of 1969/1970 and 1966/1967 salaries of a group of full-time chief executives of general purpose foundations shows that the average annual increase for members of this group in the past three or four years has been about $10,000.

Besides compensating for inflation, it is possible that the increases reflect a growing realization that the quality of a foundation's philanthropy is directly related to the quality of the people who determine where the foundation's funds will be spent. The possibility, however, is a remote one, for this concept still does not appear to be a guiding principle of foundation administration. Indeed, the study encountered founders and trustees of foundations who continue to object to spending money on salaries. They feel that such expenditure deprives a potential grantee of funds, or that people should come to foundation work because of their belief in the "cause," and not to earn a respectable salary.[3]

Given the variety of backgrounds of foundation chief executives (as shown in detail in Chapter 3), comparisons with other types of organizations is an inexact process at best. Nevertheless, because some of the larger foundations draw many of their staff from academic circles, it may be of interest to compare salary levels of presidents of universities and colleges with the salaries of foundation chief executives, and from the comparison, derive additional perspective on the latter's compensation.

Between 1969 and 1970, the median salary of presidents of colleges

---

[3] Of course, the study also encountered trustees, especially those active in the operation of a foundation, who have no objection to receiving the relatively munificent fees fixed by a trust indenture or by the courts.

and universities in the United States was $25,979, with about 11 percent receiving under $17,000, the same percent earning over $37,000, and 5 percent earning over $42,000.[4] On a frequency chart, the most often cited salary was between $25,000 and $25,500, followed, in frequency, by a salary of slightly over $30,000, and in third place, by a salary of just over $20,000.[5]

For heads of universities as for chief executives of foundations, there are large differences in salary levels. If one compares the median of college and university presidents' salaries with the averages shown earlier for heads of different types of foundations, it appears that with the exception of family supportive foundations with assets between $10 and $24.9 million and almost all types of foundations with assets of less than $10 million, full-time heads of foundations receive higher salaries than do their academic counterparts. It should be borne in mind, of course, that the college or university president in all probability receives a good many other perquisites in addition to his salary and insured benefits which the foundation executive may not enjoy, and that, on the other hand, a university president's responsibilities may be a great deal more demanding than those of most foundation heads.

Thus, although the variety of compensation levels for chief executives of foundations makes a generalization difficult, it can be said that while most foundation heads are not earning the munificent sums occasionally attributed to them, they are, by and large, reasonably well paid for their services as compared to others in somewhat analogous kinds of work. Furthermore, the current upward trend of salaries for foundation heads indicates at least an awareness on the part of foundations that there must be some movement upward in chief executives' salaries if they are to be competitive with salaries in the educational and nonprofit-organization worlds.

---

[4] It was not possible to obtain means of academic salaries.

[5] National Education Association, Higher Education Series, Research Report 1970-R, "Salaries in Higher Education," Chapter 6.

5

The Compensation Practices
of Foundations:
Staff Compensation
and Fringe Benefits

For purposes of comparison and discussion, the study's directors, as noted earlier, established ten categories of positions in addition to that of chief executive, gathering the almost infinite variety of specific titles under general labels designed to be functionally descriptive.[1] In this second chapter on compensation, the salaries of all executive staff persons other than chief executives are examined according to their categories. Also included in the discussion are such data as have been collected on the remuneration of trustees. Another section of the chapter is devoted to practices relating to fringe benefits, but here all foundation personnel is included in the discussion.

The table which follows (Table 41) shows salary ranges for people occupying next to the highest position in the various kinds of foundations. Broadly speaking, these persons, termed deputy chief executive officers by the study, discharge many of the same functions as the chief executive, sometimes covering a wide range of duties and in other cases focusing on a few aspects of the chief executive's job. Their actual titles may be vice

---

[1] For the convenience of the reader, the earlier listing of these categories in Chapter 2 is repeated. They are: deputy chief executive officer, senior secretarial officer, senior financial officer, senior secretarial-financial officer, junior secretarial-financial officer, senior program officer, junior program officer, internal administrative officer, communications/information officer, staff specialist.

Table 41. Average Salaries of Full-Time and Part-Time Deputy Chief Executives*

Percentage of time devoted to foundation	Family General Purpose	Family Supportive	Family Operating	Community	Company-Sponsored
100	$38,104 (Range: 55,000—13,800)	$11,571 (Range: 20,000—4,200)	$23,740 (Range: 40,000—7,200)	$18,500 (Range: 25,500—15,000)	$29,350 (Range: 34,700—24,000)
66–99	—	14,500 (Range: 21,300—7,200)	—	—	—
33–65	—	19,080 (Range: 40,400—3,000)	—	3,000	—
Under 33	—	4,350 (Range: 7,500—1,200) (F = 1,200)**	—	2,400	—

* In the presentation of data on the salaries of executives below the chief executive officer level, reference to asset sizes of foundations has been omitted.

** F = female. Wherever information is available, average salaries of female incumbents are shown separately.

president, associate director, executive vice president, or one of half a dozen others.

In comparing the salaries of deputy chiefs in general purpose and supportive family foundations, it is apparent that, as in the case of chief executives, the general purpose foundations provide higher salary levels but with greater ranges than are evident in the supportive foundations. Here, again, salaries seem to have little direct relation to the amount of time the person spends on the job, with instances of higher salaries for part-time than for full-time work. Incumbents of the rank of deputy chief executive in the family operating, community, and company-sponsored foundations are rare. But when these positions exist, their salaries compare favorably with those of deputy chief executives in general purpose foundations.

The next position identified is that of senior secretarial officer, usually called "secretary" by the foundation in which he or she is employed (see Table 42). Salary levels for senior secretarial staff in general purpose and supportive foundations appear to be about the same. In supportive foundations, there are a number of part-time secretaries, quite a few of whom are women. There are relatively few data on salaries of senior secretarial officers in family operating, community, and company-sponsored foundations. Such data as are available indicate that salaries of these staff members conform with those of family general purpose and supportive foundations.

In parallel posts in the financial area are individuals bearing the titles of treasurer, financial vice president, and investment manager, all of whom are grouped under the category of "senior financial officer" (see Table 43). As in the case of the senior secretarial officers, these people are concentrated in the family general purpose and family supportive foundations. Wide variations are apparent in their pay scales. This is true even in general purpose foundations where, it might be assumed, more systematic attention is given internal administrative matters and where, therefore, one would expect less variation in salaries for this office. Here, there are three instances of women receiving the lowest salary. In two other instances female incumbents are at the top of the scale.

Because the duties of secretary and treasurer are combined, in whole or in part, in some foundations, the functional title of "senior secretarial-financial officer" was assigned to such officials by the study. Since salary information on people holding this position is decidedly limited, the table on their salaries combines data for these officers in all types of foundations (see Table 44). It will be noted that individual salaries are generally on a par with those of senior secretarial and senior financial officers. Like them, moreover, they vary greatly. Officers in this category are rarely, if ever, found in company-sponsored foundations for the reason that financial af-

Table 42. Average Salaries of Full-Time and Part-Time Senior Secretarial Staff

Percentage of time devoted to foundation	Family General Purpose	Family Supportive	Family Operating	Community	Company-Sponsored
100	$27,200 (Range: 50,000–16,500) (F = 16,500)	$20,717 (Range: 37,800–8,400) (F = 16,700)	$24,166 (Range: 35,000–13,000)	—	$20,000
66–99	—	5,400	—		30,000
33–65	15,700	6,200 (Range: 25,000–1,600) (F = 3,333)	—	$9,000	—
Under 33	—	5,230 (Range: 12,000–1,400)	3,000	—	—
Unknown	—	3,933 (Range: 5,400–2,500)	—	—	—

Table 43. Average Salaries of Full-Time and Part-Time Senior Financial Staff

Percentage of time devoted to foundation	Family General Purpose	Family Supportive	Family Operating	Community	Company-Sponsored
100	$24,780 (Range: 50,000–6,000)	$20,550 (Range: 38,500–9,300) (F = 11,900)	$31,900 (Range: 32,500–31,300)	—	$20,400
66–99	20,500 (Range: 21,000–20,000)	8,100 (Range: 13,500–4,800) (F = 9,150)	—	—	—
33–65	—	10,585 (Range: 18,600–3,300)	8,100	—	—
Under 33	35,000	3,930 (Range: 10,000–1,200)	—	—	6,000
Unknown	—	10,000	7,200	—	—

Table 44. Average Salaries of Full-Time and Part-Time Senior Secretarial-Financial Staff

Percentage of time devoted to foundation	Family General Purpose	Family Supportive	Family Operating	Community	Company-Sponsored
100	$26,000	$16,616 (Range: 30,000–10,000) (F = 10,000)	$19,650 (Range: 24,300–15,000)	$10,500	—
66–99	27,500	—	13,000 (Range: 16,000–10,000)	—	—
33–65	—	9,850 (Range: 17,300–2,400)	—	—	—
Under 33	—	4,654 (Range: 15,000–1,000)	—	—	—

fairs, in this type of foundation, are almost invariably handled by officers of the sponsoring company.

A number of foundations employ a full-time or part-time junior secretarial-financial officer who works for a senior person in either area. The incumbent's title may be assistant secretary, assistant treasurer, assistant secretary-treasurer, or some other term. It is here that one finds more women officeholders than in any other executive position in the foundation world. For this reason alone further examination is justified. Also, people filling this position often carry the work load under a trustee, who has the title of secretary or treasurer but only the nominal responsibility for the functions of the office.

This is the first definitely junior position reported in these tables. Even for such a position, the salary levels seem low, especially when compared with the financial rewards of the top bracket officers and staff. The salary levels are about the same for general purpose and supportive foundations, although supportive foundations of $100 million and over usually offer more than general purpose foundations of the same size. In general, the women incumbents earn slightly lower salaries. This, interestingly enough, does not happen to be the case in supportive foundations in the $10–24.9 million asset category, where six women incumbents have a higher average salary than the overall average for men and women.

Since there are few reported salaries for this position in the other kinds of foundations, the following table again consolidates such positions for the remaining foundations other than company-sponsored foundations, which had no examples of junior secretarial-financial officers (see Table 45).

Salary data are scattered for the study's other basic classifications of foundation officers. Of the remaining categories, probably the most important and best paid is the category the study has labeled "senior program officer." The relatively high level of compensation for senior program officers is largely the result of their concentration in the larger general purpose foundations, where salary levels in general tend to be higher (see Table 46).

The salaries of senior program officers have been compared with the weighted average of salaries of full professors (in 1969–70).[2] Total compensation for full professors in certain private independent universities is $23,299, a figure that falls in the middle range of senior program officers' salaries. The weighted average salary of full professors in one hundred lead-

[2] "Weighted Average Salaries and Average Compensations by Rank, Type of Institutions, and Type of Control, 1969–70": *AAUP Bulletin*, Vol. 56 No. 2, June 2, 1970, p. 197.

Table 45. Average Salaries of Full-Time and Part-Time Junior Secretarial-Financial Staff

Percentage of time devoted to foundation	Family General Purpose	Family Supportive	Family Operating	Community	Company-Sponsored
100	$13,970 (Range: 19,500– 7,200) (F = 13,685)	$12,222 (Range: 27,700– 3,600) (F = 10,163)	$14,137 (Range: 18,500– 6,800)	$16,950 (Range: 22,000– 11,900) (F = 22,000)	—
66–99	—	5,245	9,000	—	—
33–65	—	(Range: 25,000– 1,200) (F = 5,253)	6,100 (Range: 10,000– 3,200) (F = 3,200)	—	—
Under 33	—	4,344 (Range: 10,400– 1,200) (F = 3,250)	—	3,600	—
Unknown	—	3,600	—	—	—

ing doctorate-granting institutions in 1969–1970 was $20,257.[3] This is on the low side when compared with levels of compensation of foundation program officers. It must be remembered, however, that in a great many cases, the professors can and do augment their income through outside work, whereas among foundations this practice is less accepted. Thus, apparent differences in salary levels probably are somewhat greater than variations in actual total compensation.

Junior program officers, another category set up by the study, are even more concentrated in the larger, more sophisticated foundations than are program officers of senior grade. For the junior staff, compensation data scarcely offer any basis for generalization. Nevertheless, the data, such as they are, have been tabulated (see Table 47).

A similar dearth of data exists for the remaining three categories of staff, namely, internal administrative officer, communications/information officer, and staff specialist, again, largely because they exist, if at all, among the few well-staffed, more sophisticated foundations. The first of these may bear a title such as administrative officer, business manager, or the equivalent, connoting participation in the administrative, non-program aspects of the foundation. Communications/information officers and staff specialists may be identified by such titles as director of reports, research associate or assistant, or program advisor. Examples of each of these two categories of staff are occasionally found in foundations with more than three staff members. Since salary data on staff specialists are so few, the following tabulations show data only on internal administrative officers and communications/information officers (see Tables 48 and 49).

Sources of Compensation

Information on who provides the compensation for foundation administrators is sketchy, many foundations having failed to respond to the question. Undoubtedly, some of the foundations that did not reply assumed that failure to reply would be taken to mean that the foundation was the source. If this assumption is correct, then there are relatively few foundations that look to another source than their own coffers for the wherewithal to pay the help, although, as noted below, this is probably not true of one type of foundation. In any event, of the 165 reports on who pays the chief executives' salaries, all but seven stated that the foundation paid the entire amount. Of these seven exceptions, three stated that the foundation paid

---

[3] "Weighted Average Salaries and Average Compensations by Rank and for All Ranks Combined for Selected University Sample, by Type of Control, 1969–70," op. cit., p. 197.

Table 46. Average Salaries of Full-Time and Part-Time Senior Program Officers

Percentage of time devoted to foundation	Family General Purpose	Family Supportive	Family Operating	Community	Company-Sponsored
100	$29,415 (Range: 35,000– 16,000) (F = 26,500)	$25,000 (Range: 27,500– 18,000)	$18,000	—	—
33–65	17,500	6,000	—	—	$5,000
Under 33	—	—	—	—	

Table 47. Average Salaries of Full-Time and Part-Time Junior Program Staff

Percentage of time devoted to foundation	Family General Purpose	Family Supportive	Family Operating	Community	Company-Sponsored
100	$20,678 (Range: 25,000– 11,900) (F = 12,500)	$12,500	$11,900	$11,900	—
33–65	11,300	—	—	—	—

Table 48. Average Salaries of Full-Time and Part-Time Internal Administrative Officers

Percentage of time devoted to foundation	Family General Purpose	Family Supportive	Family Operating	Community	Company-Sponsored
100	$20,000 (Range: 41,900–9,600)	$20,933 (Range: 31,700–6,100) (F = 6,100)	$26,500	—	—
33–65	20,500	—	—	—	—

Table 49. Average Salaries of Full-Time and Part-Time Communications/Information Staff

Percentage of time devoted to foundation	Family General Purpose	Family Supportive	Family Operating	Community	Company-Sponsored
100	$19,033 (Range: 28,100–14,000)	—	$15,000	—	—

between 95 and 99 percent, and the other four said the foundation was responsible for 20, 40, 50, and 75 percent respectively. The outside salary sources were the donor, another foundation, or a bank trustee. Outside sources for salaries of staff other than chief executives were equally few.

As mentioned earlier, most of the company-sponsored foundations, eighty of which were included in the study, left the salary portion of the questionnaire unanswered. It is in these foundations that one would expect to find the largest number of non-foundation financed salaries; and that expectation would undoubtedly have been confirmed had the company-sponsored foundations supplied the requisite data. The decision of the majority of the company-sponsored foundations not to answer this salary question not only deprived the study of valuable data on the financing of salaries but also prevented effective comparison of salaries paid by this type of foundation with salaries of other types of similar asset size and program activity.

Somewhat more than 8 percent of the foundations studied indicate that they allow their respective staff members to engage in compensated work outside the foundation. Since the absolute figure is fifty-four foundations, those involved consist not merely of the larger, well-staffed foundations, but also of some with decidedly small staffs. Moonlighting in the role of paid consultants to industry and government, or as editors for publishers, or as paid part-time officials of professional organizations and the like, has been characteristic of members of faculties of many universities. Apparently a small segment of the foundation world has adopted a similar liberal policy, possibly in direct imitation of the university community. Although there is no extensive evidence of the sort of "outside" work foundation staff members are performing, the presumption is that it is chiefly part-time teaching, or possibly rendering consultant services to government agencies. Indeed, some foundations (Russell Sage is one example) actively encourage their staff members to carry on a limited program of teaching at neighboring universities.

Fringe Benefits

For staff members of foundations, fringe benefits are second only to salaries in interest and concern. One foundation, the Carnegie Foundation for the Advancement of Teaching, pioneered in establishing the most important fringe benefit—an actuarially sound pension plan—for higher educational institutions. It is a matter of some irony, therefore, that, by and large, foundations have been slow, as compared with universities for example, to institute pension and other fringe benefit programs for their respective staffs. This hesitancy may be explained by a variety of factors, among them the relatively small size of foundation staffs and the absence of professional standards among foundations. Parenthetically it might be noted that some long-time observers of foundation administration and staffing practices contend that the absence of fringe benefits, commonly found in academic organizations, has been a deterrent to attracting competent staff to the foundation field. It would be impossible to prove or disprove the contention.

Of the 212 foundations that stated they had some full-time executive-level staff, 195 responded in whole or in part to the questions on fringe benefits. Of this group, 125, or about 64 percent, reported the existence of a pension plan—often the first benefit instituted by the foundation and, in some cases, the only one. Most pension plans were instituted after 1950, with a high concentration in the 1960s. Close to three-quarters of these plans are financed entirely by the foundation. Of the remaining plans, the foundation finances between 50 and 80 percent of the cost in twenty-three cases. In only thirteen plans is the foundation's share of the cost below 50 percent. If one extrapolates these data, it becomes apparent that the noncontributory pension is the rule among foundations.

In the responses to the study's questionnaires, the next most often cited benefit is major medical insurance. One hundred seven foundations stated that they have a major medical plan, while eighty-two said they did not. Following medical insurance in frequency is life insurance. Here there is an almost even split between those foundations with life insurance for their staff (ninety-five) and those without such protection (ninety-four). In the case of plans to meet hospitalization, medical, and surgical costs, such as Blue Cross and Blue Shield, reporting foundations without these benefits outnumber those having them by sizable percentages. Annual physical examinations for staff members are an even less accepted benefit, being restricted to 35 out of 188 reporting foundations. Normally, the foundation pays the full cost of all these plans.

As respects other benefits, seventeen foundations noted that they have some form of deferred compensation. Although there was no indication of the year in which deferred compensation plans were instituted, it would appear that they are of fairly recent origin and that, furthermore, there is a marked interest in such plans among foundations with more than one or two staff members. Contrary to what might be expected, only two of the foundations with such plans are company-sponsored organizations. Three are community foundations and the balance are family general purpose and supportive foundations. Eighteen foundations reported having thrift plans. These are savings plans in which the foundation matches employees' efforts to set aside part of salary as savings or offers other economic inducements to encourage such thrift. Other fringe benefits such as funds for the education of the children of staff and subsidies for staff club memberships were reported in one or two cases. Generally, the handful of the largest foundations—in asset size and/or with the most extensive staffs—have the most complete benefit package.[4]

Table 50 indicates the overall frequency of various kinds of fringe benefits within the study's universe of 662 foundations.

Table 50. Foundations Indicating Existence of Fringe Benefit Plans

	Yes	No	No Answer
Pension	125	70	467
Major Medical Insurance	107	82	473
Life Insurance	95	94	473
Blue Cross	78	111	473
Blue Shield	67	122	473
Other Medical/Surgical Insurance	36	152	474
Annual Physical Exams	35	153	474
Thrift Plans	18	172	472
Deferred Compensation	17	171	474
Disability and Accident Insurance	17	171	474
Medical Examinations after Retirement	5	183	474

The subsequent table shows the distribution of the five most usual programs, pensions, life insurance, major medical insurance, Blue Cross, and Blue Shield, among five types of foundations, classified as to asset size.

Queried as to the value of their fringe benefits as a percent of salary, the 119 foundations that answered this question fall into four fairly equal groups. Almost equal numbers indicated that the added-on value was between 5 and 10 percent (thirty foundations), between 10 and 15 percent (thirty-three foundations), between 15 and 20 percent (twenty-six foundations), and between 20 and 25 percent (twenty-five foundations). Only five foundations estimated the added-on value as being less than 5 percent. These figures support the opinion, stated earlier, that the non-contributory pension is the accepted practice among foundations which provide a pension.

Of those foundations specifying the percentage of a staff member's highest salary paid on retirement, more than half cited the figure of 50 percent or more, most of these noting that the amount was precisely 50 percent. The remaining foundations mentioned figures ranging from 1 percent to 45 percent, with the majority falling between 20 and 45 percent. In a very few cases, a formula has been devised that mixes the level of salary and years

---

[4] Benefits come in many forms. As part of its benefit program, one foundation cited the fact that the executive secretary has free parking privileges.

Table 51. Distribution of Five Important Fringe Benefits Among Five Types of Foundations

Type Foundation	Asset Size (000,000 omitted)	Pension Plan	Major Medical	Life Insurance	Blue Cross	Blue Shield
Family General Purpose	$100 & over	9	9	10	5	5
Family General Purpose	10–99.99	13	9	12	7	6
Family General Purpose	Under 10	3	4	4	2	2
Family Supportive	$100 & over	6	4	5	2	2
Family Supportive	25–99.99	15	10	10	10	10
Family Supportive	10–24.99	14	12	6	10	9
Family Supportive	Under 10	22	13	12	14	12
Family Operating	$10 & over	5	5	6	3	2
Family Operating	Under 10	11	12	12	7	5
Community	$10 & over	9	3	3	10	7
Community	Under 10	2	1	1	0	0
Company-Sponsored	$10 & over	2	5	3	1	1
Company-Sponsored	Under 10	4	4	3	2	2
Totals*		115	94	87	73	63

* For various reasons, including difficulty of incorporating some foundations in the table's classification, these totals are usually less than those shown in the listing of all fringe benefits above.

of service of the staff member, and, based on this combination, arrives at the amount of the pension. Most foundations rely entirely on the funded pension to achieve this payment, but a few find it necessary to augment the payment in order to achieve the established minimum; and to the extent that they do, the contribution must be regarded as an added fringe benefit.

As shown in the following table, most foundations provide their executive staff with four weeks annual vacation. Nineteen percent reported giving vacations of three weeks. A few provide only two weeks or offer two to four weeks depending on length of service. Seven percent are quite generous and offer more than four weeks.

Table 52. Length of Vacation Granted to Executive Staff by 195 Foundations

Number of Foundations	Length of Vacation
17	2 weeks
37	3 weeks
113	4 weeks
14	over 4 weeks
14	between 2 and 4 weeks, depending on length of service

Only six foundations reported that they have a policy of providing some form of sabbatical leave. Two said that the privilege is under consideration. The length of the leave in the few cases in which it exists varies from one to six months, every four or five years. Occasionally the amount of time given varies with the individual cases.

Compensation of Trustees

Of 540 foundations on which the study secured data on trustee compensation, 421 indicate their trustees receive no fees or other remuneration. Of the 119 foundations whose trustees do receive some form of compensation, 104 specified the range of payment. In this latter group, trustees of sixty-three foundations receive fees less than $5,000 a year. Thirty-one foundations pay their trustees between $5,000 and $20,000 annually, and ten foundations give their trustees more than $20,000. In two cases, fees exceed $50,000.[5] In many cases, the fees paid by a single foundation vary, with the bank trustees receiving a more sizable amount than the family

---

[5] Undoubtedly, there are other cases of sizable fees to trustees which were not reported to the study.

board members and other individual trustees. Or, in other cases, trustees like lawyers or accountants, who may have been selected because of their professions, receive more than their colleagues.

The magnitude of the fees paid to trustees usually depends on whether the trustees' role is that of a supervising or operating officer.[6] Of the 104 foundations on which the study secured fee ranges for trustees, 56 are trustee-operated. Their payment to trustees of fees ranging from less than $5,000 to more than $50,000 must therefore be regarded as payment for their services as operating personnel. Similar payments by 24 of the 104 foundations, classified as trustee-operated with minor assistance, must also be so regarded.

With staff increases and the consequent shift of the trustee role to one of supervision and policy determination, the payment to trustees usually declines or disappears altogether. Thus, of the foundations with full-time staff of three or less that reported to the study, only sixteen said they paid their trustees, and only eight reporting foundations with a full-time staff of more than three were among the 104 foundations that provided such compensation. In all these cases, moreover, the compensation is quite nominal—generally $5,000 or less—although one of these staffed foundations goes as high as $20,000. Usually, of course, trustees are reimbursed for travel and other out-of-pocket expenses. It is also true that individual trustees of staffed foundations, especially the board chairman or the chairman of the executive committee, may be compensated and these payments may be in the $25,000 to $40,000 range. In one case, the board chairman of a staffed foundation receives $130,000.

The 104 foundations that reported fee ranges for trustees have been tabulated (see Table 53) and an attempt made to classify them according to the absence or presence of paid staff and the magnitude of such staff when it exists. The table documents the conclusion of the analysis we have just made, namely, that compensation to trustees may rise to fairly generous levels—if there is any compensation at all—in foundations without staff and declines markedly as foundations take on staff.

Conclusions

From the welter of figures presented in this and the preceding chapter on the compensation practices of foundations, it is possible to come to at least tentative conclusions about salaries in the foundation world. It is clear

---

[6] Occasionally, when fees are fixed in a trust indenture, they may be quite arbitrary, that is, they bear no logical relationship to the role of the trustee. For additional data on trustees, see Appendix I.

Table 53. Levels of Compensation of Foundation Trustees in Foundations Classified as to Staff Size or Absence of Staff

Levels of Compensation for Trustees	Trustee-Operated		Trustee-Operated with Minor Assistance		1–3 Full-time Staff		More than 3 Full-time Staff	
	%	#	%	#	%	#	%	#
Under $5,000	53.6	30	70.9	17	68.8	11	62.5	5
5–20,000	35.7	20	12.5	3	31.2	5	37.5	3
20–35,000	7.1	4	8.3	2	0.0	0	0.0	0
35–50,000	0.0	0	8.3	2	0.0	0	0.0	0
50,000 & over	3.6	2	0.0	0	0.0	0	0.0	0
Total	100.0	56	100.0	24	100.0	16	100.0	8

that, with few exceptions, foundation executives do not receive the munificent pay that some of the public attribute to them. The salaries that are above the $50,000 level are, in most cases, those of chief executives of the large general purpose foundations, men who have major responsibilities in the administration of a professional staff and in the initiation and development of complex foundation programs. Even these are scarcely out of line with the salaries of persons of comparable intellectual stature and administrative responsibilities in government, the most prestigious universities, or in certain nonprofit organizations such as major metropolitan medical centers. The comparability of foundation salaries with those available to such persons is particularly apparent when the real income provided by certain perquisites, not usually available to foundation heads but often available to university heads and heads of certain other nonprofit agencies, are added to formal salary.

As noted earlier, some salaries for other foundation positions sustain comparison with corresponding academic levels. Thus, senior foundation program officers receive compensation approximately equivalent to that of full professors of major universities, especially if income from consulting fees and the like is averaged into the academic's salary.

Throughout this volume, the authors have commented on the American foundations' lack of pattern in their administrative practices, and particularly in matters affecting personnel. Although many compensation practices also fall within this generalization, some patterns have emerged in the data shown in this and the preceding chapter. A rough correlation appears to exist between the size of the foundation, the complexity of the job, and the remuneration of the administrator. The patterns are not neat or even always consistent, but there are enough instances of correlation of these factors in the more advanced foundations to convey the impression that the salary picture is not quite so unstructured as, for example, foundation recruiting practices.

Similarly, in the area of fringe benefits, it is apparent that, as indicated earlier, the more managerially advanced foundations with ample assets provide the greater number of benefits. Thus, as respects the five most frequently offered fringe benefits—pension plan, life insurance, major medical insurance, Blue Cross, and Blue Shield—there is a marked correlation among family-originated foundations between the type of program and the size of the benefit package, with those in the general purpose category more likely to offer a larger number of benefits than the more traditional, supportive foundations. Also, about half the foundations of all types of origin having assets of $10 million or more, which supplied data, provide the five benefits enumerated above.

To an extent, then, some sort of rough compensation pattern has emerged from the data collected by the study. It may, therefore, become possible for each of various types of foundations to find answers to some of the questions many of them posed to the study's directors. At any rate, in planning for an initial staff person, in adding to staff, or in attempting to equalize compensation for various staff levels, foundations may find it helpful to review the tabulated data and use the rough guidelines that these data suggest.

To be sure, in a constituency so lacking in institutional and administrative uniformity and so free of the pressure of professional conformity as the foundation world, it is unlikely that any compensation guidelines, however valid, will exert a commanding influence. Still, simply because the data are available and suggest generalizations as to policy, they may prove useful. They may have a measurable influence in overcoming some of the wider and less defensible discrepancies in the economic rewards of employees of different types of foundations who have similar levels of responsibility. Hopefully, also, they will at least moderate the currently unfavorable differential in income that women normally experience when employed by foundations.

6

The Foundation Administrator
Looks at His Job

Up to this point the focus has been on the factual data that relate to the foundation administrator and the institution for which he works. In analyzing and interpreting these data, policies and practices that affect foundation executive-level staff have been examined, and various aspects of the role and status of the foundation administrator have been explored in depth. These aspects have included the educational and professional backgrounds of the administrator, the way he is recruited, the work he does in a foundation, and his compensation and fringe benefits. The discussion provides an appropriate setting for an element of this inquiry to which reference has been made before but which, up to now, has not been systematically explored; namely, the attitudes and opinions that those who work, or have worked, for foundations may hold concerning their jobs and concerning foundations as places of employment.

The attitudes and opinions to be discussed are chiefly those of the 422 administrators who responded to the study's questionnaire. The positions of these respondents in the foundation world fall into one or another of the eleven job categories established by the study. One hundred fifty-six are (or were) chief executives or deputy chief executives; 171 are (or were) junior or senior program officers or concerned with program in the field; and 95 are (or were) primarily involved in a foundation's internal management or occupied a specialized staff role. Three hundred seventy-eight were employed by a foundation at the time they filled out the questionnaire. The remaining forty-four had left foundation service, about two-thirds having moved into positions in other fields of service and the remaining one-third having retired. Of those employed by foundations, about 84 percent have full-time positions, 11 percent hold part-time positions, and 5 percent failed to indicate whether their job was full- or part-time. Eighty-five percent of the respondents are male and 15 percent female. The minimum age is twenty-six, the maximum, seventy-nine, the average being about forty-nine. Five percent are under thirty and only about a quarter of the total are forty or less, a fact that confirms the conclusion that foundation service is not a mecca for youth. About 45 percent of the individual respondents reported that they have been in their present jobs five years or less; more than two-thirds reported that their tenure maximum is ten years or less. The average tenure is a little under ten years.[1]

What the Foundation Administrator Likes about His Job

In general, foundation administrators seem to be a happy and contented lot. Such an attitude is implicit, in the first instance, in the levels of satisfaction displayed by respondents when they evaluate the professional rewards their jobs supply. The mean level of ten possible sources of satisfaction identified in the study's questionnaire is 3.257 on a scale of 0 to 5.

As shown in Table 54 (and in subsequent tables), some of the sources of job satisfaction are the immediate administrative responsibilities of the job itself; other satisfactions arise from the intellectual and professional environment supplied by foundation employment; and still others come from the feeling of accomplishment that the job makes possible. Virtually

Table 54. Percentage of Foundation Staff Who Agree on the Importance of Certain Satisfactions of Foundation Service*

Satisfaction	Percentage Agreeing
Seeing money well used	82.6
Betting on good people	72.9
Association with others in foundation and related fields	59.7
Designing projects	58.2
Investigating projects	53.8
Investigating programs	52.8
Evaluating projects or programs	51.8
Evaluating applications for grants	46.7
Operating projects	31.5
Engaging in academic research	15.4

* The number of responses on which this table is based ranges from 272 to 320.

[1] For other details and discussion of possible bias as respects foundation service, either pro or con, on the part of this group of 422 respondents, see Introduction, p. 16.

all these classes of satisfactions are rated high and their relative intensity varies only slightly. In almost every case, moreover, more than half of the respondents—sometimes as many as 70 or 80 percent—agree in rating them high. Thus, the moral and social rewards that are derived from accomplishments such as "seeing money well used" and "betting on good people" are endorsed by over three-quarters of the respondents.

Rated high also are the opportunities afforded by the job to associate with others similarly motivated within the foundation field or outside. ("Opportunity to work closely with highly professional and ethical staff," was the way one respondent put it.) The formal administrative responsibilities such as the design, investigation, and evaluation of projects and programs are also satisfactions on which more than half the respondents agree. Evaluating applications for grants is a slightly less popular aspect of foundation administration, and those activities that are not too usual with foundations, such as the operation and direction of projects or engaging in academic research, have decidedly less appeal.

Nor is much difference discerned when levels of satisfaction of those from the more sophisticated foundations are compared with the satisfactions reported by individuals from foundations with few staff people. Generally, the levels coincide. Probably the only differences worth noting are the greater weight that those from the more sophisticated foundations place on project design and the greater importance that executives of smaller foundations attach to evaluating applications for grants.

The conclusion that the great majority of foundation administrators find their jobs interesting and professionally satisfying is fortified when respondents' comments on what they find especially rewarding in their foundation experience are examined. In this instance, the respondents were classified according to the job they actually held and according to their number of years of service in a foundation. What they volunteered, moreover, does not relate to the nature of their duties so much as to the intellectual and professional environment of their position and to the social impact of what they do.

As the following table indicates, the list of rewards thus volunteered is lengthy.

At the top of that list is the opportunity to carry out a creative assignment with constructive results for society. This item was cited by 21 percent. Closely related rewards, as for example, the sense of accomplishment when a grant achieves constructive results, also receive high marks. A respectable segment of respondents volunteered that they find great satisfaction in serving as entrepreneurs of ideas, in encouraging constructive ideas in others, and in associating with people, both within and outside the foundation world, who are in the vanguard when it comes to recognizing and directing

Table 55. Rewards of Foundation Service Cited by Staff Respondents to Questionnaire

Reward	Proportion of Respondents Citing Reward*	Number of Respondents Citing Reward
Opportunity to be creative and constructive and to have access to needed funds for implementing such ideas	21.1%	89
Opportunity to associate with dynamic leadership in many areas—with people concerned about being at the "cutting edge of change"	16.4%	69
Sense of accomplishment when grant produces constructive results	11.6%	49
Opportunity to be an entrepreneur of ideas	10.4%	44
Opportunity to be associated with gifted colleagues	9.2%	39
Possibility of filling social needs not filled by government or personal philanthropy	4.3%	18
Opportunity to influence prospective philanthropists to use funds constructively	4.0%	17
Special job advantages, such as absence of pressure, good remuneration, sense of power in distributing largesse, and chance to improve research specialty	4.0%	17
Opportunity to help young and talented and to follow their careers	4.0%	17
Other, including: Opportunity to become well informed on the needs and goals of educational, research, and cultural establishments Opportunity to implant or to recognize and support constructive ideas in others Opportunity to equalize opportunities for deprived minorities in our society Opportunity to improve local community	12.1%	51

* Respondents frequently cited more than one reward. Percentages given are based on total number of respondents—422.

the forces of constructive social change. Achievement of certain more specific goals such as helping the young or the disadvantaged or equalizing opportunities for minorities also receive attention as sources of professional satisfaction, although such specific objectives are cited less frequently.

Quotations of some of the actual phraseology of the respondents may convey the flavor of some of the responses: "I have enjoyed very much seeing real progress made in fields I am interested in as a result of grants I have made"; "A sense of being related to the most crucial problems of times in which we live"; "The opportunities afforded by the wide variety of responsibilities as well as full involvement in all aspects of the foundation's work is most rewarding"; "The most rewarding [aspect of the job] has been watching the seed money and what stimulation I can provide bring forth funds from other sources and involvement of many people in bringing to fruition an idea for the betterment of our community."

In addition to the specific aspects of philanthropy singled out by respondents, many participants in the study point to the pleasure, satisfaction, or reward of simply doing a job well, whether it is running the foundation, handling the finances, or carrying out some aspect of program activity. Phrases such as "guiding a new institution," "strengthening the program and financial position of the foundation," "having a large responsibility at a young age," (this from a major foundation's overseas representative), "building and leading the organization" convey this sense of a job well done. Here, one senses the professional man's or woman's satisfaction in carrying out his or her job with competence and skill.

To be sure, reactions of this kind are cited less frequently than are those involving the general goals of the organization and the environment in which the individual operates, including special conditions of foundation service that those employed in foundations find attractive. Words such as "flexibility," "freedom," and "excitement" illustrate some of the latter reactions. Some remarked that they relish the power and prestige of the job. In the words of one respondent, ". . . no one can deny the halo effect accompanying such power is ego-building and, frankly, helpful in stimulating and encouraging others to move in a given direction. I like this power."

Although heads of both general purpose and supportive foundations, program staff, and even administrative staff, appear to be of much the same mind in their opinions on the rewards of foundation service, some minor differences are evident in the opinions of those working for the thirty-five managerially advanced foundations as compared with those of staff members of the less advanced foundations. The former give higher ratings to associating with gifted colleagues (those from the smaller foundations probably *have* few colleagues), to associating with dynamic leadership and being on the "cutting edge of social change," to being in the vanguard of important ideas, and to having a generally constructive impact on society. People in the less advanced foundations tend to put greater emphasis on the opportunity foundation service affords them to help their local communities (where smaller family foundations and community foundations often are active) and on the sense of accomplishment when a grant produces constructive results.

Given the fact that association with colleagues within a foundation is often cited as a satisfying and rewarding aspect of foundation service, one would expect to find some correlation between the amount of formal and informal contact respondents feel they have and the relatively high levels of satisfaction derived from association with colleagues. This association apparently exists in satisfactory measure although its absence is a source of frustration for a few staff people (see Table 56). Respondents indicate there is frequent informal and formal contact among the staff. Heads of general purpose and supportive foundations alike have much informal contact with their staffs. In reasonably large staffs, senior program officers communicate informally with one another as do administrative officers.

What the Foundation Administrator Does Not Like about His Job

Information to complement the satisfaction data was sought by requesting opinions on the professional frustrations that foundation staffers may suffer. Sixteen possible frustrations were suggested in the questionnaire. Virtually all of them concern the management and operation of a foundation and the associations and administrative environment that a foundation may provide. None relates to frustrations that might attend efforts to achieve the professed social goals of a foundation.

The frustration levels are low—the mean for all sixteen items is only 1.269 as compared with the mean of 3.257 for the list of ten possible satisfactions. It is reasonable to assume, therefore, that respondents find more to like than to dislike in foundation work and that what they dislike, they dislike less intensely than what they like.[2]

To be sure, the very low rating given certain potential frustrations may be an indication that the respondent is merely indifferent and does not care to express an opinion on the subject. What is more likely, however, is that if a respondent takes the trouble to provide a very low rating for a suggested source of professional frustration, he is saying, in a negative way, that the situation is at least tolerable if not moderately satisfactory. Thus, it may be concluded that respondents do not find too much to criticize about foundation policy on such matters as acknowledging merit, promoting from within, encouraging writing and scholarship among staff people, and helping staff people to maintain their standing in their professional fields—all of which were given a very low rating. Although this conclusion is occa-

---

[2] A further reason for the lower levels on this issue of dissatisfactions than on the question of satisfaction is the *response set,* or the general tendency of respondents to questionnaires to give lower ratings to negative questions or statements. This should be considered in evaluating negative appraisals.

sionally contradicted by comments offered in another context, it is probably fair to conclude that the frustration level in these matters is insignificant.

The only possibly significant levels of dissatisfaction that were expressed concern administrative standards and procedures within the foundation, and a few of these might well be considered by those concerned with improving foundation administration. Thus, the highest frustration level is reserved for the failure of a foundation to evaluate performance and measure what it does. Crowding this weakness are such other administrative weaknesses as an overabundance of paper work, lack of care in investigating proposed philanthropic investments, insufficient foundation contact with projects the foundation may be financing, unwillingness to invest in projects likely to pay off only over the long term, and a tendency of the foundation to support projects of a favored trustee or staff member.

A comparison of the levels of frustration of people from the more sophisticated foundations with those from less sophisticated foundations shows that in all cases, frustration levels of people working for the former are higher. In most cases, to be sure, the differences are extremely small—

Table 56. Percentage of Foundation Staff Respondents Citing Certain Professional Frustrations

Frustration	Percentage Citing Frustration*
Lack of evaluation procedures for completed projects	30.3
Too much administrative paper work	29.4
Insufficient time to develop long-range projects	25.8
Superficial investigation and appraisal of projects or programs	23.3
Insufficient time to associate with projects financed by the foundation	22.2
Tendency of foundation to support special philanthropic interests of favored trustees or staff member	17.9
No opportunity to initiate or design projects	12.5
Lack of professional association with others in foundation field	9.6
Lack of knowledge of or experience with projects financed by the foundation or problems to which foundation addresses itself	9.0
Preemption by trustees of the designing and investigative responsibility for most important projects	7.4
Inability to maintain place in professional field or discipline	7.1
Too little intellectual stimulation	6.9
Difficulty in communicating ideas to trustees	6.7
Insufficient contact with superior or head of foundation	6.6
Lack of encouragement of outside writing or research	6.1
Nepotism	3.1

* The number of responses on which these percentages are based ranges from 272 to 347.

one- or two-tenths of a point—but in three areas, there is a more substantial difference. Close to one-and-a-half times as many people from the advanced foundations feel that trustees tend to preempt important projects. The frustration with administrative paper work is measurably more in the advanced foundations, as is the feeling that there is not enough contact between the staff person and the head of the foundation.

One can speculate about the reasons for these differences. In the case of the preemption by the trustees of administrative work on projects, it might be assumed that, in the major foundations, there is more developmental work to be done, and that a staff is hired with special competence to do this work. Thus, encroachment by the trustees into staff functions is resented. In the less advanced foundations, on the other hand, an active role by trustees is often the normal and accepted way of operating, and because most of these foundations confine themselves largely to making grants to other institutions, there is less in the way of developmental work for anyone to do. The other two frustrations concerning paper work and contact with the head of the foundation bespeak a multi-staff situation rather than a one- or two-person office.

It is, perhaps, appropriate at this juncture to refer briefly to the thesis of Frederick Herzberg that job satisfactions and dissatisfactions are not opposite poles of the same dimension, but rather are two different dimensions, a view that is largely corroborated by respondents. Herzberg says that the characteristics of a job that relate to satisfactions are intrinsic elements of the job that satisfy the need of the jobholder for achievement, recognition for achievement, work itself, responsibility, and advancement. All of these relate to a person's job functions rather than the situation or environment in which the functions are carried out.

Dissatisfactions or frustrations, on the other hand, stem from what Herzberg says are extrinsic elements that satisfy what he terms the "hygienic" needs of the individual, needs affected by the employing organization's policies and administration, the nature of supervision, salary, interpersonal relations, and working conditions. Thus, a person may be both satisfied with the intrinsic elements of his job and dissatisfied with certain environmental factors. Herzberg writes, "A good hygienic environment can prevent job *dis*satisfaction, but cannot create true job satisfaction or happiness" (author's italics).[3]

Judging from responses to the study's questionnaires, most respondents are satisfied with both intrinsic and extrinsic elements of their jobs, or if they do feel dissatisfied with certain extrinsic factors the internal satis-

[3] Frederick Herzberg, "Motivation, Morale and Money," *Psychology Today*, March, 1968, Vol. 1, No. 10, p. 45.

factions they find on the job normally outweigh environmental annoyances.

The relatively high degree of satisfaction that the foundation administrator exhibits toward the conditions of his employment and its rewards rises to an even higher level when attitudes on his economic status are examined. Only 28.2 percent of respondents to the question indicated that their salary was in any way unsatisfactory. (On a scale of 0 to 5, the mean rating given to dissatisfaction with salary level is 0.759.) Other possible sources of economic dissatisfaction such as the absence of economic incentives, unsatisfactory fringe benefits, and the lack of a provision for salary review received mention from an even lesser number.

If responses from staffs of the two different groups of foundations are again compared, some distinctions between the two groups' reactions on these economic issues emerge, although neither group is seriously concerned. Those from the less advanced foundations express a greater degree of dissatisfaction with all aspects of their economic condition than their counterparts from the more advanced foundations. Thus, 28.2 percent of the less advanced foundation group express some degree of displeasure with their fringe benefits. Twenty-three percent are critical of the absence of salary review, and 30.4 percent are unhappy to one degree or another with their salary. On each of these three issues significantly smaller percentages from the more advanced foundations expressed displeasure.

Table 57. Comparison of Attitudes on Economic Issues of Staffs of Advanced and Less Advanced Foundations

	Staff of Managerially Advanced Foundations	*Staff of Other Foundations*
Unsatisfactory salary	27.2%	30.4%
No provision salary review	14.0%	23.1%
No economic incentives	18.3%	23.8%
Unsatisfactory fringe benefits	12.9%	28.2%

If any doubt remains that foundation people, as a whole, like their jobs, that doubt is dispelled by the replies made to rather bluntly phrased questions on how they compare their jobs with others and as to whether they would exchange their present positions for something else. Fifty-six percent of 377 respondents say their jobs in a foundation are more rewarding than those held by people in other fields of endeavor; 37 percent are unwilling to commit themselves on the issue, one way or another; and only 7 percent feel that jobs outside the foundation field might be more attractive.

Within the foundation field itself, 75 percent (of a total of 375 respondents) prefer their own foundation over any other as a place to work. About 70 percent of these are of the opinion that their job satisfactions are greater than those of other foundation employees. Forty-one percent (of 393 respondents) take the cautious stance that they cannot be sure or do not know whether their satisfactions are greater than those of employees of other foundations, and only 9 percent feel that employees of other foundations enjoy a more satisfactory professional life.

When asked whether they would consider giving up their existing foundation assignment for another, over 90 percent (315 out of 340 respondents) say they prefer to remain with their present foundation and that they do not wish to move to another foundation. About 7 percent of the respondents would consider moving out of the foundation field altogether, but since this question is phrased in a hypothetical manner, so necessarily is the answer. About a third of these say they might consider a teaching or administrative post at a college or university, and about a fourth say they might consider returning to their former profession or business.

The tenacity with which most foundation employees seem to want to cling to their respective jobs is not entirely consistent with other data revealed by the study. As indicated in Chapter 3, in the four years prior to 1970, 299 foundation people did indeed leave the field, but this outward movement seems not to have been precipitated by a rejection of foundation service *per se*. Rather as already suggested, it seems to have resulted from incompatibility with the views of a new foundation head or changing foundation programs, or from both considerations.

Future Foundation Service

One of the concerns of the study was to elicit opinions from the foundation constituency on how foundation service might be made more attractive and on what attracts others to such service. Out of the responses, it was hoped, might come constructive suggestions for improving foundation administration and improving also the process by which individuals are brought into the service of foundations. Respondents were asked to offer suggestions on these points, chiefly through responses to specific questions. The responses illustrate the ambivalence of practitioners who are reasonably content with the *status quo* and do not particularly care to "rock the boat" and yet feel obligated, when requested to do so, to react to suggestions of possible constructive changes.

As respects the matter of improving foundation service, the following table places some stress on certain administrative improvements, although the suggestions do not appear to be backed with much enthusiasm. Some favor is shown the suggestion that foundations institute a kind of sabbatical leave policy comparable to that in vogue in universities, a practice, which, it will be recalled from the earlier discussion on fringe benefits (Chapter 5), six foundations said had already been instituted and two that it was being considered. The idea is measurably more popular with staff members of the better staffed foundations than with their counterparts from the less advanced foundations. For the latter group, many of whom are the sole executives of their organizations, the idea would not be feasible for the obvious reason that there is no one to whom the daily operations of the foundation could be delegated. Another suggestion that is reasonably popular with respondents is that staff should enjoy a greater involvement in designing and administering projects. Support for this suggestion is almost evenly divided between respondents from the greater foundations and respondents attached to the lesser foundations. On the other hand, only a moderate amount of enthusiasm is displayed for other suggestions for improving the conditions of foundation service and thus making it more attractive. An appropriate tabulation follows in Table 58.

Respondents were also asked to identify aspects of foundation service which, in their opinion, make such service attractive to others and presumably encourage them to seek to enter such service. It is noteworthy that respondents from both the more advanced and the lesser foundations regard "opportunity to perform a public service" as the aspect of foundation

Table 58. Percentage of Foundation Staff Who Agree on Relative Importance of Each of Suggested Ways of Making Foundation Service More Attractive

Suggested Change	Percentage Agreeing*
Something like a sabbatical	48.9
Greater involvement in designing and administering projects	41.7
Leave granted for special research/writing	36.4
Promotion from within	32.7
Additional foundation-financed training for staff	27.1
Loan of personnel to other foundations or organizations	23.5
Transforming grant-making foundations into operating foundations, in part at least	22.7
Foundation encouragement of participation in professional meetings	21.4
Greater economic rewards	18.8
Special economic incentive for outstanding accomplishment	17.1
More generous and comprehensive fringe benefits	12.1
Greater job security, including tenure	10.3

* The number of responses on which each of these percentages is based ranges from 294 to 333.

activity which would exert the greatest influence in attracting others to foundations. Though percentages varied somewhat as respects the attracting power of other, more specific, forms of service, such as "influencing" a given field of interest, experimenting with social reform, or aiding the underprivileged, respondents from both groups of foundations rated each of these very high.

As respects the attracting power of opportunities in foundations for personal development, there was agreement among respondents of the two groups of foundations that foundation employment afforded a means of gaining a position of respect in one's professional field or in one's community and that this would enhance the attractiveness of such employment. On the other hand, there were marked differences between the two on the subjects of travel opportunities and the opportunity to develop in one's special discipline or profession, the respondents from the major foundations rating each of these much higher than the respondents from the other foundations. For obvious reasons, greater opportunity for personal intellectual advancement in one's discipline or profession is normally offered by the more advanced, project-oriented foundations; it is therefore not surprising that staff people in these foundations regard such an opportunity as an aspect of foundation employment which would attract outsiders. As for travel opportunities, the well-staffed foundations are more likely to require travel and provide the necessary back-up staff for it than the foundations with one or two people in charge. Again, therefore, it is not surprising that respondents from the more advanced foundations should place greater emphasis than respondents from other foundations on the appeal exerted by travel opportunities in a foundation job.

In discussing the attractions of foundation service and ways to improve it, respondents occasionally, and quite logically, touched upon the much broader question of the training and recruitment of foundation personnel, a subject discussed at some length in Chapter 3. As indicated in that chapter, there is no persuasive evidence that the foundation community wishes to make any radical changes in the *ad hoc* practices presently in vogue for discovering talent, identifying appropriate training, and inducting new personnel into the foundation field. One explanation for this apparent lack of desire to systematize the process of recruitment is the hesitancy exhibited toward the concept of a professional foundation career service.

As we have already noted, there are various reasons for this hesitation. One is the variety of training and experience that a foundation seeks or that different foundations demand. Another is the fact that, as foundation programs change, new kinds of skills and training may be called for. Another is the strong belief that philanthropy, as practiced by founda-

**Table 59. What Attracts Others to Foundations? The Views of Staffs of
Managerially Advanced and Less Advanced Foundations**

Elements Attracting Others to Foundation Service	Percentage of Staff of 35 Advanced Foundations*	Percentage of Staff of Other Foundations†
Opportunity to perform public service	74.6	78.9
Opportunity to influence given field of interest	69.2	53.3
Opportunity to experiment with social reform	54.2	43.7
Opportunity to aid underprivileged	50.5	53.3
Opportunity to gain respected position in professional field and community	45.9	45.5
Opportunity to encourage growth in professional field or discipline	40.9	26.9
Professional association with like-minded individuals	39.8	40.6
Opportunity to foster intellectual research and development in the young	32.9	41.0
Opportunity to gain wider public and professional recognition	32.9	34.0
Opportunity to travel	30.9	14.0
Financial rewards	24.9	18.5
Opportunity to apply contemporary technology to education and research	15.5	7.7

* The number of responses from the advanced foundations on which each of these percentages is based ranges from 233 to 256.
† The number of responses from the less advanced foundations on which each of these percentages is based ranges from 91 to 114.

tions, is not something that can be learned—that it is not, and never can be, a specialized body of knowledge such as, for example, exists in the law or in branches of medicine. Still another is the belief that certain qualities of mind and personality are more valuable in foundation service than any formal training. In short, greater standardization in these matters and the establishment of professional norms, are ideas that inspire relatively little enthusiasm among foundation administrators.

Suspicion of professionalism is, at least by implication, reiterated in the responses which some administrators made to the questionnaire addressed to them, and their opinions strengthen the case against viewing foundation service as a profession, outlined earlier in Chapter 3. For one thing, as noted earlier, they are clearly hostile to any kind of tenure guarantee. This attitude may merely reflect the existing *de facto* security of most foundation jobholders. On the other hand it probably also reflects uneasiness

118 / The Foundation Administrator

on the part of some that the tenacity with which most foundation employees cling to their jobs and the rather high average age level of administrators are not good for foundations, and further, that if this propensity to cling were to be reinforced by tenure guarantees, the result might be distinctly unacceptable to the more socially alert critic.

Some respondents enlarge on the reasons for their hostility to tenure. In so doing, they reiterate the difficulty of reconciling the concept of a foundation career service offering permanent tenure with the obligation of foundations (as they interpret it) to lead the forces of change and develop new ideas. Most of them, therefore, cover much the same ground already covered in Chapter 3 but their testimony is, nevertheless, worth recording. If foundations are to serve the public properly, say these respondents, they need a constant infusion of new ideas. This condition, they suggest, can be realized most effectively by curtailing tenure, sending older hands into new areas of activity, and bringing new faces into foundations. One respondent says quite bluntly that "a foundation official should be someone whose main allegiance is elsewhere." Others reiterate a radical view formulated earlier on these pages, namely, that after a minimum term of service in a particular foundation, most staff people should move on to other pursuits. Carrying these views to their logical conclusion, one chief executive noted that his foundation had abolished tenure in order to give the foundation greater flexibility in changing its programs, and with its programs, its staff. The reader may conclude, quite rightly, that the ideal revealed in these views is quite inconsistent with the fact of rather limited movement in the foundation world revealed earlier. The reader may also be reminded that this is not the first time that ideological implications and practice have diverged.

Opinions on Impact of 1969 Tax Reform Act

Related to this issue of how foundation administrators can improve their identification with the changing aspirations and needs of society is the context of governmental regulation and policy in which the future administrator will perforce have to carry on his work. An effort was made to secure the opinion of the foundation community on this issue. This effort centered upon the 1969 Tax Reform Act. The result was touched upon in Chapter 1. Here, the issue is more thoroughly explored.

Of 320 respondents, about 51 percent think the impact of the act will be generally negative—that foundation service will become less attractive as a result of it. Twenty-three percent think there will be no difference, and 13 percent feel that foundations will be better places in which to work as a result of the legislation. Two percent said it was too soon to tell, and 11 percent said they don't know.[4]

Of those who believe the impact of the legislation will be positive—and there are only forty-one respondents with this view—almost half of them (44 percent) think the legislation will create a demand for more skilled staff. The professionals in greatest demand, they say, will be lawyers. People with specialized program knowledge and writing and journalistic training will tie for second place. There will also be an increased demand for individuals with business and accounting experience.

Of the 157 respondents who feel that the recent legislation will make foundation service less attractive and who are willing to give their reasons, 46 percent of them think that the 1969 Tax Act will inhibit innovation, especially in social and political spheres. Somewhat more than a third of this group (36 percent) believe that the result of the new law will be greater complexity in foundation administration, more government control, more red tape, or more routine chores. About a tenth of this group think foundations in the future will be less prestigious places in which to work.

Representatives of less advanced foundations are more certain than their counterparts in the major foundations that the new legislation will make foundation administration generally more complex. A greater percentage of respondents of the more advanced foundations, however, are convinced that the new law will inhibit innovations in programming. Some of these staff members from the major foundations say foundations will become more attractive to the more cautious, that flexibility will be impeded, especially in foreign countries, and that, in the words of one respondent, "a basically conservative institution of American society will tend to become more conservative."

If opinions on the positive or negative impact of the new legislation are classified according to the principal job responsibility of the respondents, one finds that those in administrative positions have the highest percentage of positive views—about 24 percent of the people in these positions. Twenty-one percent of heads of supportive foundations share these positive

---

[4] Representatives of the less advanced foundations are more decided than staff members of the more advanced foundations in both their optimism and their pessimism about the future of foundation service. Twenty-five percent of the respondents from the less advanced foundation group think foundation service will be more attractive, while only 8 percent from the more advanced foundations take this view. Fifty-four percent from the less advanced foundations think foundation service will be *less* attractive, whereas in the case of the major foundations 48 percent think it will be *less* attractive. A higher percentage of those from the major foundations than of those from the lesser foundations feel the law will have no effect either way.

views. The high figures for those who think the effect of the legislation will be negative are found among junior program people (54 percent), senior program personnel and heads of supportive foundations (53 percent, in each case), and heads of general purpose foundations (50 percent). As respects the opinion that the legislation will have no impact the percentage ranges from a high of 30 percent among senior program people who responded to the questionnaire to a low of 14 percent among heads of mainly supportive foundations. Junior program officers, administrative staff, and heads of general purpose foundations tend to share the opinion of senior program officers on this point.

Inserted almost parenthetically in the discussion of the impact of recent governmental regulation were a few comments on a problem that perennially plagues foundations and is of prime importance in their relations with government and society. This is the relative lack of comprehension by the public of what foundation administrators do to earn their paycheck. Although the administrator says he does not feel misunderstood, his confidence that others have an accurate perception of his job is certainly not unmixed with doubt. In reply to the question: "Do you feel that people outside the foundation understand your work?" only 19 percent answer unequivocally "yes." Forty-two percent of 385 respondents say they are understood most of the time. Thirty-five percent feel such understanding is rare. The different kinds of foundations, the variety of functions they perform, and the small number of people employed in the field undoubtedly all contribute to the feeling on the part of the administrator that others do not wholly understand his work. In written comments appended to questionnaires and in conversations, individual foundation executives emphasize the uniqueness of their foundation and, by extension, the uniqueness of their work. Clearly here is an area in which foundation specialists can and should do intensive thinking if the administrator and his employer are to survive and thrive.

In a time characterized by a general sense of malaise and by much, and often bitter, criticism of various professions and institutions, including foundations, it is in many ways gratifying to be able to report on such a comparatively well satisfied group of executives as described in this chapter. Obviously the overwhelming majority of foundation administrators like their jobs. Their morale is high. They like what they do and how they go about doing it. Generally, they approve of the conditions under which they operate and the results they attain in contributions to social welfare. All this is indeed gratifying and should be a source of comfort not only to those who, like the directors of the study, have the opportunity of reporting these attitudes, but also to the entire foundation community.

At the same time such a report can also be disconcerting, if not disquieting. To those outside the foundation fold, and especially to those who have been critical of foundations in recent years, such an affirmative report on attitudes can raise questions the answers to which may not be wholly agreeable to the foundation constituency. For such critics the report may well suggest that the typical foundation administrator is too complacent about his role and cause them to question whether he is really alert to the contemporary demands on the philanthropy which foundations administer. In a world in which almost every day sees the unveiling of another unmet need in our society, should not one expect to find a greater degree of impatience with the *status quo* among foundation executives and a more critical view of their role as public benefactors?

7

Conclusions and Outlook

Although the foundation has been the object of several earlier studies focusing on such aspects as its trustees, its investments, and its relations with government,[1] this study is the first to undertake a systematic examination of those who administer foundations. In it some attention has been given to foundations that operate without paid staff and rely on paid or unpaid trustees. But the study's principal aim has been to provide reliable data, as well as comment reinforced by the data, about the contemporary, paid, foundation administrator. These data include his training and background, the way in which he is recruited, the nature of his activities, his direct and indirect compensation, his attitude toward his work, his satisfactions and frustrations, his conception of his role in various types of foundations, and the way in which different kinds of foundations avail themselves of his services.

Earlier chapters have examined each of these aspects of the status and role of the administrator, analyzed and interpreted the relevant data, and offered appropriate conclusions. At the risk of some repetition, these concluding pages attempt to provide a profile of the administrator based on these findings. Occasionally, where warranted, trends that may affect the future of the administrator are interspersed in the analysis. Special consideration is given to the evidence offered by the study as to existing and

---

[1] The following are some of the volumes involved: Donald R. Young and Wilbert E. Moore, *Trusteeship and the Management of Foundations*, 1969; Ralph L. Nelson, *The Investment Policies of Foundations*, 1967; Marion R. Fremont-Smith, *Foundations and Government*, 1965; F. Emerson Andrews, *Legal Instruments of Foundations*, 1958, and *Philanthropic Foundations*, 1956; and Eleanor K. Taylor, *Public Accountability of Foundations and Charitable Trusts*, 1953. All these studies were published by Russell Sage Foundation.

future staffing expectations for foundations and the ways in which these expectations may influence the future role and status of the foundation administrator.

Some Highlights of the Administrator Profile

As noted in Chapter 3, the employed foundation administrator undergoes one of many kinds of education and training and comes to his foundation post from many different professions and occupations. The popular stereotype that the administrator is a former academician is confirmed only to the extent that there are more former academicians in foundation service than representatives of any other profession or occupation. Indeed, if a hypothetical aspirant for foundation service were to try to plan for a career in philanthropy, he would be hard put to know where to start. For despite the fact that a majority of the study's individual respondents indicated they came from four professions or vocations, their entry into foundation service was marked by an element of adventitiousness. Of 298 respondents, only ten said that they in any way planned or prepared for foundation service.

To repeat a statement made with some frequency in this report, there is only a limited opportunity for the specialist in the foundation community. By and large, foundations are still havens for the "generalist." Judging from the data collected on the background of respondents, a generalist may come from almost any professional or occupational group. He may be an educator, a lawyer, a bank officer, an editor, or a government servant. By definition, his training is not necessarily related to any particular foundation's program. Rather, he is an individual wise in the ways of the world and shrewd in evaluating the motives and abilities of his fellows. Often, the important factor in his consideration for foundation service is the fact that he knew someone in, or connected with, a foundation at the time it was seeking staff.

Although the reign of the generalist is not likely to end soon, the demand for the specialist may be expanding. The likelihood of such an expanded demand will be enhanced if the more advanced foundations become increasingly concerned with the origination and design of projects and programs and, above all, with monitoring and evaluating them. For such activities, foundations will require specialists—specialists, that is, in particular program areas or disciplines and not necessarily in foundation administration *per se*. In these cases, however, there may be increased use of consultants rather than of permanently employed staff, because any subsequent change in program brought about by changing social demands, by the interests or background of a newly appointed chief executive, or by a changing board majority, creates the problem of a staff specialist no longer relevant to program and therefore expendable.

It must be reiterated that nothing resembling a trend toward the specialist is apparent even among the most sophisticated foundations. Among them, as among the generality of foundations, warm regard continues to be expressed for the traditional amateur type of foundation executive. Nor, as stated earlier, is there any serious expectation that preparation for, and entry into, foundation service will soon become more institutionalized and systematic than the practices reviewed in these pages. A principal reason is that much of the criticism of the present *ad hoc* method of operation comes not from the foundation community itself but from critics outside foundations. For the observer inside the foundation world, prevailing practices seem appropriate to the continuing reliance on the non-specialist administrator, and hence that observer rarely voices doubts about the *status quo*.

Turning to the study's findings about the appraisals and attitudes of the people who serve staffed foundations, the data show that in general, their morale is high. As discussed in some detail in Chapter 6, most respondents like the actual functions they perform, the content of their work, and the overall goals of their foundation, as well as their surroundings and compensation. Many took the trouble to comment on the sense of fulfillment that association with a foundation has provided. High levels of satisfaction were displayed both by veterans of twenty years or more service and by those who had been in their present job less than a year.

Unquestionably, the spirit of service to others reported in the study is as compelling a force for many foundation executives as it is for ministers, teachers, missionaries, and others devoted to the cause of advancing the welfare of their fellowman. Indeed, further sociological research might bring to light a number of similarities between the backgrounds and motivations of foundation administrators and ministers of a few generations past. The foundation administrator might be included in the band of secular ministers of today—particularly those who are drawn to work for the public good but who, in general, prefer to maintain some distance between themselves and the objects of their concern.

The same sense of fulfillment provided by foundation service was expressed by most of those who had left foundations for other pursuits. Many retired foundation executives evidently look back with a sense of exhilaration over what they feel they accomplished in serving the causes of social progress and the advancement of knowledge. Of those who left prior to retirement age, the study indicates that dissatisfaction with the job was not the cause of their departure. The reason in most instances, as has already been suggested, was a change in the philanthropic policies or programs of the foundation—possibly caused by a change in leadership—with the result that the individual's knowledge and skills were no longer in demand. The sense of satisfaction with foundation service was indeed so high that the authors expressed qualms as to whether the contemporary foundation administrator might be altogether too content for one who is supposed to be on the intellectual and social firing line.

To be sure, qualifications of this prevailing sense of satisfaction with foundation service did occasionally manifest themselves, although the dissatisfactions rarely concerned the social role of the foundation administrator—at least not directly. Moreover, the dissatisfactions expressed were considerably less intense than the satisfactions. Approximately two-thirds of the study's respondents expressed some degree of frustration over the following four aspects of program administration: investigation of projects, evaluation procedures, developmental work on projects, and design of long-range projects. The fact that respondents offered any criticism at all in these areas indicates that interest in greater involvement in the program function is by no means restricted to a few specialists in the largest foundations.

If these dissatisfactions were to become more intense than they are at present, they might have the effect of propelling the mature foundations more rapidly into directly designed and administered philanthropy and of at least nudging the supportive foundations toward some initiating and designing activities. The pressure for change, however, will have to be considerably more acute before these rather faint signals become a beacon illuminating a discernible trend.

In discussing their dissatisfactions with foundation employment, surprisingly few respondents touched upon discrimination for reasons of race or sex. Their silence on the subject was due in part to the imperfections of the study questionnaire and, in part, and probably chiefly, to the low concentration of women and minority people in foundation executive positions. Most foundations with blacks on their staff have added them only recently, despite the organizations' professed, and usually sincere, concern for the welfare of the black minority and the creditable record that some foundations made even prior to World War II in tackling minority problems.

As for women, the foundation employment record is no better than that of the business world and certainly not so good as that of the institutions of higher education in which, in 1969, women held 22 percent of the faculty and other professional staff positions.[2] Only one or two foundations

---

[2] See chart in "Underutilization of Women Workers," Women's Bureau, Workplace Standards Administration, United States Department of Labor, Washington, 1971, p. 10 (Chart F).

that can be considered of major size have a woman chief executive. There is the usual and frequently hidden discriminatory salary and promotion policy, with the resultant, all too frequently justifiable, complaint that women do the work and men reap the kudos and the monetary rewards. With token exceptions, the world of the staffed foundation is still a white world and a man's world, and this fact does not appear to cause too serious concern among those who govern and manage foundations.

Because foundation administration is so unstructured, it is possible to overemphasize the unique and the idiosyncratic and to ignore occasional evidence of uniformity or, at least, of similarity. Such evidence does exist, and there are even occasional patterns. As was pointed out in Chapters 4 and 5, there is some similarity in the pay scales of particular levels of administrators employed by foundations with similar programs and asset sizes. There is also a fair degree of similarity in practices relating to fringe benefits and to retirement policies.

There are similarities as well in the kinds of responsibilities discharged by administrators. Indeed, within foundations supporting similar types of programs, the duties of administrators are probably more alike than different. Especially is this true of personnel of reasonably well-staffed foundations, where functions have become somewhat departmentalized. It is also true of the personnel of the small, one-to-three-staff, supportive foundations who are normally involved in all of a foundation's activities, both those of a program nature and those relating to the foundation's internal management and its financial affairs.

On the whole, however, the similarities that exist are largely accidental. Any profile such as this chapter tries to delineate must remain loose and lacking in homogeneous components. The import of the study's data is that virtually every facet of the administrator's job is unstructured. Whether it be the preparation for the job, the constituency from which he is recruited, the way in which he is recruited, the kinds and levels of responsibility assigned him, and to a considerable extent, the level and nature of his compensation, variation, rather than uniformity, prevails. In all these matters, professional norms are lacking. *Laissez faire* seems to be the mood of the foundation universe and idiosyncratic treatment the rule.

These variations and differences in the administrator's status and role result chiefly from the fact that foundation administration is not a profession—at least not yet—and that the administrator is not a member of a professional corps with established norms or accepted standards that make for a greater degree of uniformity and standardization. Indeed, until recently, the contemporary administrator lacked even the forums, associations, and the like through which he might overcome some of these variations in his job, explain his role to government and the public, talk with colleagues in his field, and receive and offer counsel on problems of common concern, including the problems relating to his role and status.

The Outlook for Staffing

As previously intimated, the durability of the amateur tradition in private philanthropy may offer some explanation for this condition among the administrator constituency. Chiefly, however, the condition results from the small size of the administrator population. A universe of less than fifteen hundred individuals is simply too limited numerically to establish the critical mass necessary to identify a professional group and exert serious influence on status and role. Moreover, this difficulty, inherent in the paucity of numbers in the administrator universe, is aggravated by the distribution of that universe. As already noted, more than 52 percent of the full-time membership of that universe inhabit thirteen major project-oriented foundations. Among these foundations, program activities and the general scale of operations are such that they require rather specialized personnel, persons with training and experience and with an outlook on philanthropy quite different from the administrator who staffs the lesser, more supportive, or conduit type of foundation. Then, too, administrators of the latter type of foundation are often alone in managing a foundation, or at best they have one or two colleagues. They operate in not so splendid isolation from their fellows in other foundations, and communication is difficult even if they had enough in common to benefit from such communication.

Happily, as already intimated something is being done to mitigate the traditional isolation of the foundation administrator and overcome at least this obstacle to a more professional outlook. Relatively well-structured meetings like the biennial conference on charitable foundations at New York University, the varied agenda of the annual conferences of the Council on Foundations and the National Council on Philanthropy, regional associations of foundations in the Southwest and more recently in the Southeast, and group meetings, informal seminars, and luncheons of foundation executives and staff people held in metropolitan centers like New York City illustrate the change.

These developments are making it increasingly possible for even the most isolated foundation administrator to exchange ideas with other administrators, to discuss problems and goals common to many foundations, to consider with others the changing role of private philanthropy, and even to mount concerted attacks with other foundation administrators on a particular problem within a metropolitan or regional area. In this process of bridging the void among administrators, The Foundation Center has been an especially constructive influence. It has become so by disseminating reliable data on foundations and their activities, by identifying those who serve as foundation administrators or trustees, and by urging foundations to become more responsive to the need of providing the public with hard data about themselves and those whom they employ.

These developments, however desirable, are at best melioristic. They do not go to the root cause of the administrator's isolation and the relative absence of professional values. That root cause continues to be the miniscule number of administrators and their distorted distribution pattern. Unless and until there is at least a modest increase in the number of those who earn their livelihood in foundations, and unless and until a majority of full-time administrators are distributed among more than thirteen foundations, there is little likelihood of any major change in the professional status of foundation administration. In turn, such expansion and more even distribution depend upon the willingness of more foundations currently run by the trustees to go into the market for staff. They also depend on the willingness of other foundations, especially those of major asset size, at present operating under a skeletal management of one or two employees, to expand staff to a respectable size.

Some observers are optimistic as to the possibility of such expansion of foundation personnel. Their optimism is based on the alleged awareness of foundation people that some of the difficulties in which foundations have recently found themselves with government and the public are traceable in no small measure to the absence of staff or inadequate staffing. With no one to tend store, many foundations have been unable to discharge even the most elementary administrative responsibilities. In far too many cases, there has been no one to establish operating standards that would pass muster with the most indulgent student of administration; no one to compile, write, and distribute a public report; no one to provide the hard data about the foundation for appropriate reference volumes or for those making legitimate inquiry. Optimists on staffing believe that these weaknesses have become so obvious that they can no longer be ignored.

Others, also optimistic about expanded future staffing, take the position that the foundation community's leadership, now intent on creating a better public and governmental image of foundations, will exert maximum pressure on at least the larger less-developed foundations to provide staffing adequate to insure compliance with the new federal tax, pay-out, and accountability legislation. The efforts of these leaders to establish a national agency to speak to government and the public for the foundation world will, it is observed, scarcely achieve the intended objectives unless a great many more foundations with substantial assets, foundations which at present are little more than addresses in a post office, lawyer's office, or a bank, establish administrative headquarters of their own, hire some permanent full-time employees, and begin to act like responsible organizations.

Still other proponents of staffing take comfort from the hope that some of the smaller foundations, whose endowments do not generate enough income to warrant employment of individuals on a permanent full-time basis may begin to take advantage of proposals to consolidate resources in order to justify staffing or to share personnel with other foundations. The proposals take a variety of forms. They include consolidation of foundations on a regional basis, the association of the local community foundation and small family foundations within a given community, the operation of one foundation by another, a liquidating grant of assets by a smaller to a larger foundation, and various arrangements by which two or more foundations share the time of paid administrators. As noted earlier, some of these proposals have reached the experimental stage, although the study found little enthusiasm for either the experiments or any untried proposals of this nature, and hence found little to justify the hopes of those who look to such moves as a means for more extended foundation staffing.

Finally, proponents of foundation staffing see expanded opportunities for would-be foundation administrators arising from the normal institutional evolution of certain foundations and their resulting managerial requirements. Over the years, as the asset value increases and family and donor influence decreases, some foundations move up from the stage where they served merely as a conduit for family charities into what might be called an intermediate stage of development, and still later to a more project-oriented type of program. Even at the intermediate stage, giving, although still of the conduit or supportive type, becomes more sophisticated. It is likely to include large grants to scientific, medical, and similar research institutes and bureaus, to educational institutions, to scholarship and fellowship agencies, and to other organizations that serve as distributing agents for the foundation or the foundation's "retailer." Hence, even at this stage foundations are likely to acquire some expert help and, of course, once the foundation goes to the next stage and establishes itself at a level where it seeks to design and, to some extent, direct its own program, considerable specialized help is required. Although relatively few foundations may be affected by this evolutionary process, examples can be provided of some that have undergone such development or are currently experiencing such an evolution. The observation that this growth cycle provides a kind of natural demand for staff is not without merit.

Considerations such as the foregoing may therefore point toward a greater use of staff by American foundations, and in time, they may lead to a general improvement of the staffing picture. In time, too, this may produce a more professional type of employee than the profile of the administrator provided in this report.

At the same time, it must be said that data and observations on the issue of future staffing revealed by the study offer little cause for optimism about expanded foundation staffing and a more professionally oriented corps of administrators. In the first place, it is apparent that most of the traditional restraints on staffing, reviewed in Chapter 1, continue as potent forces to discourage this development. Almost without exception, respondents from trustee administered entities stated that they saw no need for paid staff, that the donor or trustees or other amateurs and volunteers conducting the foundation's business were adequate, and that a paid staff would constitute an undesirable intrusion.

A second, less explicit rejection of staffing, but equally unpromising for staffing in the long term, is the implication of the kind of program activity supported by respondents. Whatever validity there may be to the suggestion made earlier that there is a natural maturation process affecting foundations that leads to increasing program and managerial sophistication and hence to a need for expert staff, the fact is that the responding foundations, by and large, are quite content with their essentially conduit role. As noted in Chapter 1, 68 percent of all foundations questioned see their role as a supportive one. Only the barest fraction—slightly over 1 percent— define their role as one in which the foundation undertakes responsibility for identifying priorities and becomes involved in designing and elaborating projects and in maintaining contact with the project's administration. Just under 15 percent identify themselves as combining supportive and innovative activities. Hence program outlook and managerial needs among the generality of foundations, as revealed by the study's data, provide little hope either for a surge in staffing, or even for a modest bulge, or for a professional corps of administrators.

Respondents concerned with improving and expanding staffing also pinned some of their hopes on the tax legislation of 1969, but, as already remarked, other respondents indicated such hopes are unlikely to be realized except in rather specialized and not always desirable ways. As respects staffing, the new legislation probably has spurred interest in persons who would attend to the household and internal managerial duties of certain foundations—what might be labeled "protective staff." It is quite probable that some foundations will come to the market for staff to take care that new federal regulations on foundation taxation, pay-out, and reporting are properly observed and that no legal liability attaches to either the foundation or to trustees or staff whom the tax legislation euphemistically identifies as "foundation managers."

On the other hand, the penalties that may be imposed for violating certain legal limitations of a qualitative nature that affect program activity will almost certainly make foundations more conservative and less innovative than heretofore and confirm their already pronounced tendency to content themselves with conventional supportive or conduit philanthropy. Assuming such a result, the legislation can only have the effect of discouraging program staffing. Certainly, it will place a premium on program activity that can most easily dispense with staff and inhibit the kind of activity that at once requires a degree of program expertise and that appeals to the talented and trained program candidate.

These pessimistic views on future staffing received a degree of statistical confirmation from the responses by the queried foundations to specific questions about initial staffing and additional staff. It will be recalled that of the total queried universe of foundations, only thirty-four said that they had hired their first full-time administrator during the previous four years, and four said they contemplated such a move in the oncoming year. These were greatly outnumbered by other responding foundations, which indicated that they contemplated no move in the direction of enlarging a miniscule staff or hiring the initial staff member. Actually, the total number of entirely new staff that foundations said they had added or would add (thirty-eight), is about 9 percent of the total of people who were reported as having been promoted from within or brought in from the outside to take care of normal turnover during the last five years.

At best, therefore, the outlook as to future foundation staffing and a higher degree of professionalization that might result from increased staffing, is a mixed one. Although there has been some improvement among a group of the more progressive foundations, the vast bulk of foundations, including many with sizable assets, have not been persuaded that what they do or plan to do requires the services of someone who makes the management of philanthropy an activity from which he earns his livelihood. Nor is anything approaching a breakthrough in staffing likely to occur unless and until a much larger fraction of foundations of size deliberately change to a more sophisticated philanthropic role than they currently support. Only if major aggregates of foundation wealth become serious about transforming the foundation from its conventional supportive or conduit role into an instrument of social and intellectual change—only if they become more serious about their traditional but scarcely honored claim to be social pioneers and frontiersmen in the world's search for new knowledge and innovations in applying that knowledge—will the staffing situation change significantly and for the better. Should that kind of change take place, the expert foundation administrator would not be expendable as he is now, and his tribe would increase. At the same time, without raising too dogmatically the issue of professionalism, some of the confusion and debate that currently attends discussion about his background and preparation, about how he is to be sought out, how employed, and how rewarded, would begin to clear up.

The Immediate Prospect

It is a truism that foundations and the people who staff them cannot be considered apart from the society in which they operate. In a time characterized by economic recession, increasingly vocal minorities of the right and left, and a generally conservative political atmosphere in the country at large, many institutions may find themselves hewing to a course that has been tried before and with which they are familiar. It is not a time for innovation, and foundations, peculiarly sensitive to trends of this nature and peculiarly vulnerable, are especially influenced by the prevailing spirit of the times.

Chastened, and in some cases frightened, by the 1969 Tax Reform Act, many foundation administrators apparently aim to create as few ripples in the social pond as possible in carrying out their programs. Thus, while some experimenting may take place, the next few years would seem to be a time when most foundations will try to "play it safe." Such a prediction is echoed by a former foundation executive who, in corresponding with the study's directors, forecast that "foundations will pay more attention to 'blue chip' organizations" in selecting their donees. Changes undoubtedly will take place, perhaps more rapidly than now anticipated. The 1970s, however, would seem to be a period of consolidation for foundations, of waiting to interpret the mood of the country and the government. The suspicion is that it will not be a mood calculated to encourage experiment and innovation, or the hiring of staff eager and equipped to design and develop programs in this mold.

On the other hand, it is possible that, for the short term at least, the very existence of this study and the conclusions to which it has come regarding foundation staff will cause some foundations to place a greater premium on competent professional help. The study's findings may persuade some unstaffed foundations of moderate size to undertake at least the minimum staffing required to discharge any organization's basic administrative obligations. Other unstaffed or only nominally staffed foundations, currently emerging as foundations of considerable asset size, may be influenced to establish a level of staffing consistent with their increasingly sophisticated managerial and program demands. Should this happen, the funds invested in the study and the time and effort which many individuals have contributed to it will have been justified.

Appendix I

A number of frequency listings and cross-tabulations produced by the study were not incorporated in the text, either because the data were unessential or wholly irrelevant to the discussion, or because the data and their analyses were technically unacceptable. Some of these data, imperfect though they may be, may still be of interest to the reader. In cases in which this seemed likely, these data, usually tabulated and preceded by a brief description or explanation, have been incorporated in this Appendix.

Administrative Costs

The first of the following two tables seeks to relate foundation administrative costs to volume of annual grants (1969). Eight ranges of annual administrative costs, with a minimum of $1,000 and a maximum exceeding $1 million, are cross-tabulated with seven grant aggregates, the minimum being less than $100,000 annually, the maximum over $20 million. The table is based on data from 348 foundations.

Administrative costs as a percent of grant volume show great variations—so much so that such percentages have little significance. It may be noted that somewhat over half of the foundations fall into the two grant volume categories ranging from $100,000 to $1 million and that, among them, the largest number of foundations in any one grant-administrative-cost combination in the table is thirty-seven. For any foundation in this group of thirty-seven that approaches maximum in grant volume and administrative costs, the administrative cost is 5 percent of grant volume.

If the same assumptions are made for each of the next highest numbers of foundations (thirty-three and thirty-two) in this general area of the table, the resulting administrative costs, as a percent of grant volume, are 6.6 percent and 2 percent.

For the four foundations in the table with the highest administrative cost budgets and the largest grant volumes (again using maximum), administrative costs are about 5 percent, although clearly costs run higher in the case of these foundations—probably, in some cases, well over 10 percent.

At the other end of the spectrum are six foundations within the lowest range of administrative costs ($1,000–$5,000) that make between $1 and $3 million in grants annually. For them, of course, administrative costs in relation to grant volume are infinitesimal. These are foundations that have no paid staff (see Table 60).

Table 61 also deals with administrative costs but seeks to relate them to staff size. Seven staff levels, ranging from none to 100 or more, are cross-tabulated with eight levels of reported administrative costs (as of the fiscal year 1969). As in the previous table, the administrative costs range from a level of $1,000–$5,000 to a level in excess of $1 million. The number of foundations involved is 359.

Three-fourths (75.7%) of the foundations fall into the four administrative cost categories ranging from $6,000 to $200,000. Of these the great majority (68 percent) either have no executive staff or have not more than one or two full-time staff members.

Although three-quarters of all foundations that report the lowest range of administrative costs ($1,000–$5,000) have no staff, there are sizable numbers of foundations without staff in the higher administrative cost categories, for example, six foundations in the $200,000–$500,000 cost category and two in the $500,000 to $1 million cost category. These are obviously foundations that provide their trustees with generous fees.

As is to be expected, with minor exceptions, foundations with staffs of even modest size fall into the upper ranges of the administrative cost categories. Thus twenty-four foundations that employ from three to ten full-time staff members report costs that range from $200,000 to over $1 million; those that employ from eleven to one hundred or more report costs that in most cases are over $500,000. In five cases the cost exceed $1 million and in at least two of these cases the excess over $1 million is probably considerable.

Although cost computations based on the number of staff are probably more meaningful than costs based on grant volume, neither procedure is particularly helpful if the analyst is trying to arrive at cost standards. Variables such as the fees paid trustees and especially the kind of program supported by the foundation make the derivation of such standards virtually impossible (see Table 61).

Substantive Program Areas Favored by Foundations

Foundations were asked to indicate the relative favor shown various substantive program areas by rating them on a scale from 0 to 5. The following list of program areas provides the percentage of the more than 600 foundations studied that gave any area a rating of 4 or 5 (Table 62).

Miscellaneous Data on Foundation Trustees

A few of the data reproduced here have already appeared in the text. For the convenience of the reader they are repeated along with other data relating to trustees that have not appeared elsewhere (Table 63).

Table 60. Eight Possible Levels of Foundation Administrative Costs Cross-Tabulated with Seven Possible Ranges of Grant Dollar Volume

Administrative Costs	$1–99	$100–299	Grant Dollar Volumes (000 omitted) $300–999	$1,000–2,999	$3,000–5,999	$6,000–19,999	Over $20,000	Total
$1,000–$5,000	10 22.7%	6 8.3%	16 11.9%	6 10.0%	1 4.8%	0 0.0%	0 0.0%	39 11.2%
$6,000–$20,000	18 40.9%	33 45.8%	32 23.7%	6 10.0%	1 4.8%	0 0.0%	1 33.3%	91 26.2%
$21,000–$50,000	8 18.2%	19 26.4%	37 27.4%	12 20.0%	5 23.8%	0 0.0%	0 0.0%	81 23.3%
$51,000–$100,000	5 11.4%	9 12.5%	26 19.3%	13 21.7%	1 4.8%	0 0.0%	0 0.0%	54 15.5%
$101,000–$200,000	2 4.5%	4 5.6%	15 11.1%	12 20.0%	3 14.3%	1 7.7%	0 0.0%	37 10.6%
$201,000–$500,000	0 0.0%	0 0.0%	6 4.4%	8 13.3%	8 38.0%	5 38.4%	1 33.3%	28 8.0%
$501,000–$1 million	1 2.3%	1 1.4%	3 2.2%	2 3.3%	2 9.5%	4 30.8%	0 0.0%	13 3.7%
More than $1 million	0 0.0%	0 0.0%	0 0.0%	1 1.7%	0 0.0%	3 23.1%	1 33.4%	5 1.5%
Total	44 12.7%	72 20.7%	135 38.8%	60 17.2%	21 6.0%	13 3.7%	3 0.9%	348 100.0%

Table 61. Seven Possible Staff Levels (Including One for Foundations without Staff) Cross-Tabulated with Eight Possible Levels of Foundation Administrative Costs

Staff Levels	Administrative Costs (000 omitted)								Total
	$1–$5	$6–$20	$21–$50	$51–$100	$101–$200	$201–$500	$501–$1,000	Over $1,000	
None	29	52	28	7	9	6	2	0	133
	74.4%	54.8%	34.1%	12.7%	22.5%	20.0%	15.4%	0.0%	37.1%
1	6	34	35	18	10	3	1	0	107
	15.4%	35.8%	42.7%	32.7%	25.0%	10.0%	7.6%	0.0%	29.8%
2	1	7	13	18	7	4	0	0	50
	2.5%	7.4%	15.9%	32.7%	17.5%	13.3%	0.0%	0.0%	13.9%
3–5	3	1	5	10	10	12	4	0	45
	7.7%	1.0%	6.1%	18.2%	25.0%	40.0%	30.8%	0.0%	12.5%
6–10	0	1	0	2	2	4	4	0	13
	0.0%	1.0%	0.0%	3.7%	5.0%	13.3%	30.8%	0.0%	3.6%
11–100	0	0	1	0	2	1	2	4	10
	0.0%	0.0%	1.2%	0.0%	5.0%	3.4%	15.4%	80.0%	2.8%
Over 100	0	0	0	0	0	0	0	1	1
	0.0%	0.0%	0.0%	0.0%	0.0%	0.0%	0.0%	20.0%	0.3%
Total	39	95	82	55	40	30	13	5	359
	10.9%	26.5%	22.8%	15.3%	11.1%	8.4%	3.6%	1.4%	100.0%

Table 62. Program Areas Favored by Foundations

Area	Percent Rating 4 or 5
Education	39.9
Individual and family welfare	28.5
Community action or services	22.9
Health and medicine	20.7
Capital grants for schools, hospitals, museums, or community facilities	13.3
Arts	11.0
Religion	10.4
Scholarships, fellowships, aid to individuals	8.4
Science and technology	5.9
Social sciences	4.8
Community ethnic or interracial relations	4.4
Recreation	4.0
International affairs	2.5
Conservation	2.3
Humanities	2.1
Foundation administration-maintenance of special projects or programs	1.6
Manpower training and employment	1.5
Civil rights	1.4
Housing	1.4
Population research	0.9
Political process	0.8
Organization of philanthropic activities	0.2
Government, law, etc.	0.2

Table 63. Size of Boards of Trustees

Number of Foundations	Number of Board Members
117	5
101	3
75	7
65	4
60	6
39	9
33	8

Other foundations reported higher numbers of trustees, including one foundation with forty, but the average of all reporting foundations was six. As indicated in the text, 135 foundations said that the chief executive officer serves on the board *ex officio*. This is 93.7 percent of the 144 foundations that responded to this particular question.

Table 64. Frequency of Board Meetings

Number of Foundations	Frequency of Meetings
91	More often than quarterly
76	Quarterly
59	Twice a year
34	Once a year
33	Three times a year
29	On call

In addition a number of foundations reported that their Board meets at set times and on call when necessary.

Table 65. Role of Trustees

Number of Foundations	Philanthropic Role
438	Determine foundation policy
407	Ratify or deny projects
398	Discuss projects in detail
226	Originate projects
165	Amend and develop projects
	Financial Role
125	Delegate financial and investment matters to one trustee
115	Study and authorize investment changes
108	Delegate most investment responsibility to investment counsel
86	Delegate most investment responsibility to bank or trust officer

Table 66. Role of Trustee Committees

Number of Foundations	Type of Committee	Committee Role	Percent of Foundations
81	Trustee–Staff Committee	Makes recommendations to full Board	77.7
		Reviews and evaluates projects	65.4
		Screens requests for grants	64.1
106	Trustee Committee	Makes recommendations to full Board	58.4
		Makes recommendations on finance/investments	48.1
		Screens requests for grants	43.3
		Reviews and evaluates projects	42.4
101	Executive Committee	Operates in lieu of Board	77.2
		Makes preliminary appraisals of projects	32.6
72	Executive Committee includes operating officers		33.3

In evaluating most of the above data, readers are reminded that many of the foundations studied are trustee-operated and have no staff. The role of these trustees is therefore quite different from that of trustees of staffed foundations.

Appendix II

This Appendix consists of salary tables in somewhat greater detail than those provided in the text. The latter are the result of considerable consolidation and "collapsing" of the tables reprinted here. One of the advantages of these more detailed tables is that they list salaries for staffs of foundations of various asset sizes.

(1) *Chief Executives*

**Table 67. Salaries, Full-Time and Part-Time Chief Executives
Family General Purpose Foundations**

Average Salary	Range High	Range Low	% Time	Asset Range Foundation (in millions of dollars)
$57,250	$75,000	$40,000	100	100 & over
60,000	——	——	66–99	100 & over
30,000	——	——	33–65	100 & over
45,625	72,000	25,000	100	10–99.9
12,500	15,000	10,000	33–65	10–99.9
20,000	——	——	Under 33	10–99.9
28,400	——	——	100	Under 10
32,500	35,000	30,000	66–99	Under 10
11,000	——	——	Under 33	Under 10

Table 68. Salaries, Full-Time and Part-Time Chief Executives Family Supportive Foundations

| Average Salary | Range | | % Time | Asset Range Foundation (in millions of dollars) |
	High	Low		
$27,333 (F = $15,000)*	$34,100	$15,000	100	100 & over
28,000	——	——	66–99	100 & over
37,000	——	——	33–65	100 & over
36,746 (F = 25,700)	60,000	16,400	100	25–99.9
40,000	——	——	66–99	25–99.9
29,360	50,000	5,600	33–65	25–99.9
8,266	15,800	3,000	Under 33	25–99.9
40,000	——	——	Unknown	25–99.9
20,150 (F = 18,000)	40,000	7,500	100	10–24.9
18,000	——	——	66–99	10–24.9
15,933	50,000	7,500	33–65	10–24.9
4,500	10,000	900	Under 33	10–24.9
10,000	——	——	Unknown	10–24.9
17,650 (F = 16,200)	40,000	1,700	100	Under 10
12,200 (F = 16,000)	18,000	6,000	66–99	Under 10
11,438 (F = 7,400)	20,000	4,800	33–65	Under 10
6,585 (F = 5,500)	16,000	3,000	Under 33	Under 10
8,025	12,500	1,200	Unknown	Under 10

* F = female. Wherever information is available, average salaries of female incumbents are shown separately.

**Table 69. Salaries, Full-Time and Part-Time Chief Executives
Family Operating Foundations**

Average Salary	Range		% Time	Asset Range Foundation (in millions of dollars)
	High	*Low*		
$33,800 (F = $30,000)	$45,000	$25,000	100	10 & over
12,000	——	——	33–65	10 & over
22,207 (F = 4,600)	45,000	4,600	100	Under 10
13,000	20,000	6,000	66–99	Under 10

**Table 70. Salaries, Full-Time and Part-Time Chief Executives
Community Foundations**

Average Salary	Range		% Time	Asset Range Foundation (in millions of dollars)
	High	*Low*		
$26,463	$40,000	$18,200	100	10 & over
27,000	34,000	20,000	66–99	10 & over
8,900	18,000	7,000	33–65	10 & over
6,500	10,000	3,000	Under 33	10 & over
11,500	25,000	3,600	100	Under 10
4,200	——	——	66–99	Under 10
8,533 (F = 2,400)	18,000	2,400	33–65	Under 10
800	——	——	Under 33	Under 10
2,400	——	——	Unknown	Under 10

Table 71. Salaries, Full-Time and Part-Time Chief Executives Company-Sponsored Foundations

Average Salary	*Range*		*% Time*	*Asset Range Foundation (in millions of dollars)*
	High	*Low*		
$31,700	$55,000	$16,100	100	10 & over
26,250	35,000	17,000	66–99	10 & over
18,225	27,000	8,000	100	Under 10
32,166	40,000	26,500	66–99	Under 10
6,000	——	——	33–65	Under 10

(2) *Deputy Chief Executives*

Table 72. Salaries, Full-Time and Part-Time Deputy Chief Executives Family General Purpose Foundations

Average Salary	*Range*		*% Time*	*Asset Range Foundation (in millions of dollars)*
	High	*Low*		
$44,025	$55,000	$23,300	100	100 & over
29,863	40,000	13,800	100	10–99.9
33,000	——	——	100	Under 10

**Table 73. Salaries, Full-Time and Part-Time Deputy Chief Executives
Family Supportive Foundations**

Average Salary	*Range* High	*Range* Low	*% Time*	*Asset Range Foundation (in millions of dollars)*
$16,666	$20,000	$15,000	100	25–99.9
35,200	40,400	30,000	33–65	25–99.9
14,500	21,300	7,200	66–99	10–24.9
8,333	11,000	3,000	33–65	10–24.9
7,500	——	——	Under 33	10–24.9
7,025	8,400	4,200	100	Under 10
15,000	——	——	66–99	Under 10
2,950 (F = 1,200)	6,000	1,200	Under 33	Under 10

**Table 74. Salaries, Full-Time and Part-Time Deputy Chief Executives
Family Operating, Community, and Company-Sponsored Foundations**

Average Salary	*Range* High	*Range* Low	*% Time*	*Type Foundation*	*Asset Range Foundation (in millions of dollars)*
$40,000	$ ——	$ ——	100	Fam. Op.	10 & over
19,675	32,500	7,200	100	Fam. Op.	Under 10
17,333	21,000	15,000	100	Community	10 & over
2,400	——	——	Under 33	Community	10 & over
25,000	——	——	100	Community	Under 10
3,000	——	——	33–65	Community	Under 10
29,350	——	——	100	Co. Spon.	Under 10

(3) *Senior Secretarial Officers*

Table 75. Salaries, Full-Time and Part-Time Senior Secretarial Officers Family General Purpose Foundations

| Average Salary | Range | | % Time | Asset Range Foundation (in millions of dollars) |
	High	Low		
$33,200	$50,000	$23,000	100	100 & over
15,700 .	——	——	33–65	100 & over
21,750 (F = 16,500)	27,500	16,500	100	10–99.9
25,000	——	——	100	Under 10

Table 76. Salaries, Full-Time and Part-Time Senior Secretarial Officers Family Supportive Foundations

| Average Salary | Range | | % Time | Asset Range Foundation (in millions of dollars) |
	High	Low		
$28,000	$35,000	$20,000	100	100 & over
19,928 (F = 20,200)	29,200	10,000	100	25–99.9
14,500 (F = 25,000)	25,000	4,000	33–65	25–99.9
3,000	——	——	Under 33	25–99.9
21,800 (F = 15,600)	37,800	12,000	100	10–24.9
2,400 (F = 1,800)	3,000	1,800	33–65	10–24.9
5,933	10,000	1,800	Under 33	10–24.9
2,500	——	——	Unknown	10–24.9
15,775 (F = 10,800)	25,100	8,400	100	Under 10
5,400	——	——	66–99	Under 10
3,950 (F = 4,100)	6,000	1,600	33–65	Under 10
5,250 (F = 1,400)	12,000	1,400	Under 33	Under 10
4,650	5,400	3,900	Unknown	Under 10

Table 77. Salaries, Full-Time and Part-Time Senior Secretarial Officers Family Operating Foundations, Community Foundations, and Company-Sponsored Foundations

Average Salary	Range High	Low	% Time	Type Foundation	Asset Range Foundation (in millions of dollars)
$35,000	$ ——	$ ——	100	Fam. Op.	10 & over
18,750	24,500	13,000	100	Fam. Op.	Under 10
3,000	——	—	Under 33	Fam. Op.	Under 10
9,000	——	——	33–65	Community	Under 10
20,000	——	——	100	Co. Spon.	10 & over
30,000	——	—	66–99	Co. Spon.	Under 10

(4) *Senior Financial Officers*

Table 78. Salaries, Full-Time and Part-Time Senior Financial Officers Family General Purpose Foundations

Average Salary	Range High	Low	% Time	Asset Range Foundation (in millions of dollars)
$27,560	$50,000	$15,600	100	100 & over
20,000	——	——	66–99	100 & over
35,000	—	——	Under 33	100 & over
22,000	33,000	6,000	100	10–99.9
21,000	—	——	66–99	10–99.9

Table 79. Salaries, Full-Time and Part-Time Senior Financial Officers Family Supportive Foundations

| Average Salary | Range | | % Time | Asset Range Foundation (in millions of dollars) |
	High	Low		
$30,000	$ ——	$ ——	100	100 & over
18,600	——	——	33–65	100 & over
20,871	38,500	11,400	100	25–99.9
(F = 13,200)				
10,400	——	——	33–65	25–99.9
8,100	13,500	4,800	66–99	10–24.9
(F = 9,150)				
7,500	10,000	5,000	Under 33	10–24.9
14,650	20,000	9,300	100	Under 10
(F = 9,300)				
8,675	13,000	3,300	33–65	Under 10
3,037	7,400	1,200	Under 33	Under 10
10,000	——	——	Unknown	Under 10

Table 80. Salaries, Full-Time and Part-Time Senior Financial Officers Family Operating Foundations and Company-Sponsored Foundations

| Average Salary | Range | | % Time | Type Foundation | Asset Range Foundation (in millions of dollars) |
	High	Low			
$31,300	$ ——	$ ——	100	Fam. Op.	10 & over
32,500	——	——	100	Fam. Op.	Under 10
8,100	——	——	33–65	Fam. Op.	Under 10
7,200	——	——	Unknown	Fam. Op.	Under 10
20,400	——	——	100	Co. Spon.	10 & over
6,000	——	——	Under 33	Co. Spon.	Under 10

(5) Senior Secretarial-Financial Officers

Table 81. Salaries, Full-Time and Part-Time Senior Secretarial-Financial Officers Various Types of Foundations

Average Salary	Range High	Range Low	% Time	Type Foundation	Asset Range Foundation (in millions of dollars)
$26,000	$ ——	$ ——	100	Fam. Gen. Purp.	100 & over
27,500	——	——	66–99	Fam. Gen. Purp.	100 & over
15,400	——	——	100	Fam. Supp.	100 & over
17,300	——	——	33–65	Fam. Supp.	100 & over
30,000	——	——	100	Fam. Supp.	25–99.9
6,500	——	——	33–65	Fam. Supp.	25–99.9
15,000	——	——	Under 33	Fam. Supp.	25–99.9
14,500	17,500	10,000	100	Fam. Supp.	10–24.9
2,400	——	——	33–65	Fam. Supp.	10–24.9
4,166	5,900	3,100	Under 33	Fam. Supp.	10–24.9
10,800	——	——	100	Fam. Supp.	Under 10
13,200	——	——	33–65	Fam. Supp.	Under 10
3,386	9,400	1,000	Under 33	Fam. Supp.	Under 10
10,000	——	——	66–99	Fam. Op.	10 & over
19,650	24,300	15,000	100	Fam. Op.	Under 10
16,000	——	——	66–99	Fam. Op.	Under 10
10,500	——	——	100	Community	10 & over

(6) Junior Secretarial-Financial Officers

Table 82. Salaries, Full-Time and Part-Time Junior Secretarial-Financial Officers Family General Purpose Foundations

Average Salary	Range High	Range Low	% Time	Asset Range Foundation (in millions of dollars)
$15,330 (F = 16,800)	$19,300	$10,800	100	100 & over
12,733 (F = 12,700)	19,500	7,200	100	10–99.9
11,500	——	——	100	Under 10

Table 83. Salaries, Full-Time and Part-Time Junior Secretarial-Financial Officers Family Supportive Foundations

Average Salary	Range		% Time	Asset Range Foundation (in millions of dollars)
	High	Low		
$24,566 (F = 18,300)	$27,700	$18,300	100	100 & over
7,300	——	——	33–65	100 & over
3,825 (F = 3,500)	4,800	3,500	Under 33	100 & over
12,900 (F = 11,850)	15,000	10,500	100	25–99.9
16,650 (F = 25,000)	25,000	8,300	33–65	25–99.9
3,000	——	——	Under 33	25–99.9
9,385 (F = 10,116)	13,700	4,700	100	10–24.9
3,944	6,000	2,100	33–65	10–24.9
8,380 (F = 4,550)	14,000	3,600	100	Under 10
3,600 (F = 2,750)	8,000	1,200	33–65	Under 10
5,200	10,400	1,200	Under 33	Under 10
3,600	——	——	Unknown	Under 10

Table 84. Salaries, Full-Time and Part-Time Junior Secretarial-Financial Officers
Family Operating Foundations and Community Foundations

Average Salary	Range		% Time	Type Foundation	Asset Range Foundation (in millions of dollars)
	High	Low			
$17,500	$18,000	$17,000	100	Fam. Op.	10 & over
5,700	5,900	5,300	33–65	Fam. Op.	10 & over
10,775	18,500	6,800	100	Fam. Op.	Under 10
9,000	—	—	66–99	Fam. Op.	Under 10
6,600	10,000	3,200	33–65	Fam. Op.	Under 10
(F = 3,200)					
16,950	—	—	100	Community	10 & over
(F = 22,000)					
3,600	—	—	Under 33	Community	10 & over

(7) *Senior Program Officers*

Table 85. Salaries, Full-Time and Part-Time Senior Program Officers Various Types of Foundations

Average Salary	Range High	Range Low	% Time	Type Foundation	Asset Range Foundation (in millions of dollars)
$29,877	$35,000	$22,800	100	Fam. Gen. Purp.	100 & over
17,500	17,500	17,500	33–65	Fam. Gen. Purp.	100 & over
21,433	30,000	16,000	100	Fam. Gen. Purp.	10–99.9
24,200	——	——	100	Fam. Gen. Purp.	Under 10
27,500	——	——	100	Fam. Supp.	25–99.9
25,000	——	——	100	Fam. Supp.	Under 10
6,000	——	——	33–65	Fam. Supp.	Under 10
18,000	——	——	100	Fam. Op.	Under 10
5,000	——	——	Under 33	Co. Spon.	Under 10

(8) *Junior Program Officers*

Table 86. Salaries, Full-Time and Part-Time Junior Program Officers Various Types of Foundations

Average Salary	Range High	Range Low	% Time	Type Foundation	Asset Range Foundation (in millions of dollars)
$20,795 (F = 12,500)	$25,000	$12,500	100	Fam. Gen. Purp.	100 & over
11,300	——	——	33–65	Fam. Gen. Purp.	100 & over
14,950	18,000	11,900	100	Fam. Gen. Purp.	10–99.9
17,000	——	——	Unknown	Fam. Gen. Purp.	10–99.9
14,600	——	——	100	Fam. Gen. Purp.	Under 10
12,500	12,500	12,500	100	Fam. Supp.	25–99.9
11,900	12,900	11,000	100	Fam. Op.	Under 10
11,900	——	——	100	Community	10 & over

(9) *Internal Administrative Officers*

Table 87. Salaries, Full-Time and Part-Time Internal Administrative Officers Various Types of Foundations

Average Salary	Range High	Range Low	% Time	Type Foundation	Asset Range Foundation (in millions of dollars)
$25,750	$ ——	$ ——	100	Fam. Gen. Purp.	100 & over
20,500	——	——	33–65	Fam. Gen. Purp.	100 & over
14,250		——	100	Fam. Gen. Purp.	10–99.9
20,000	——	——	100	Fam. Gen. Purp.	Under 10
31,700		——	100	Fam. Supp.	100 & over
25,000	——	——	100	Fam. Supp.	25–99.9
6,100	——	——	100	Fam. Supp.	Under 10
26,500	——	——	100	Fam. Op.	Under 10

(10) *Communications/Information Officers*

Table 88. Salaries, Full-Time and Part-Time Communications/Information Officers Various Types of Foundations

Average Salary	Range High	Range Low	% Time	Type Foundation	Asset Range Foundation (in millions of dollars)
$21,050	$28,100	$14,000	100	Fam. Gen. Purp.	100 & over
15,000	——	——	100	Fam. Gen. Purp.	10–99.9
15,000	——	——	100	Fam. Op.	10 & over

Appendix III

Reproduced on the following pages are the two original study questionnaires used. The first was sent to the foundations studied and the second to individual foundation administrators.

The Study of the Foundation Administrator

It is realized that not all of the following questions will be applicable to your foundation. Where none of the given alternatives within a question applies to your situation, it would be appreciated if you would make full use of the "Other (please specify)" category. If an entire question has no application to your foundation, would you please write "not applicable" or "N.A." after the question?

Explanation of terms:

Executive-level employees are defined as those who participate, to any degree, in decision-making functions. The term *foundation administrator* is used synonymously with "executive-level staff member."

1. Official name of foundation and date of founding as trust or corporation:

   Name_____ Date of founding_____

2. Market value of assets as of December 31, 1969 . . . . $_____

3. Annual number and dollar volume of grants for the last two years:

Dollar Volume	Number
1968_____	_____
1969_____	_____

   Please indicate the dollar amount of your largest grant in the last two years $_____

   Please estimate the percentage of the dollar value of all grants and other appropriations allocated to each of the following:

   Organizations in the United States . . . . _____%

   Individuals in the United States . . . . _____%

   Organizations or individuals outside the United States . . . . _____%

   Projects directly administered by the foundation in the United States and abroad . . . . _____%

   Other (Please specify)_____%

4. What is the total of your foundation's administrative budget for 1968 and 1969? (If your foundation is partially an operating organization, please omit costs attributable to directly administered projects.)

   1968 _____ 1969 _____

5. Please rate (from 0 to 5) *each* of the following areas of grants in relation to your foundation's activities during the past two years.

   Education . . . . _____
   (Research and instruction in teaching methods and administration; libraries.)

   Services in support of individual and family welfare . . . . _____
   (Family assistance, youth and child welfare.)

   International affairs . . . . _____
   (Individual and institutional assistance in any field outside the U.S.; disarmament; international political and economic relations, law, and administration.)

   Health and medicine . . . . _____
   (Research, education, and clinical training)

   Science and technology . . . . _____
   (Physical and life sciences—research and technical applications)

   Religion . . . . _____
   (Church support, religious education, etc.)

   Social sciences . . . . _____
   (Education and research.)

   Humanities . . . . _____
   (Literature, philosophy, history, classics, and languages.)

   Arts . . . . _____
   (Performing arts and fine arts)

   Community action or services . . . . _____
   (Community improvement)

   Recreation . . . . _____
   (Programs and sites)

   Conservation . . . . _____
   (Natural resources, pollution control, ecological research)

   Manpower training and employment . . . . . _____
   (Vocational training, retraining, research on manpower problems.)

   Community ethnic or interracial relations . _____

   Civil rights . . . . _____
   (Research, legal defense, etc.)

   Housing . . . . _____
   (Design, construction, financing, etc.)

   Political process . . . . _____
   (Voter registration, civic education.)

   Other (Please specify)_____

6. How would you characterize the program of your foundation? (Please check)
   a. Supportive, i. e. engaged in giving grants for the general support of existing institutions...........☐
   b. Concerned with initiating, designing, and counselling on research and investigative
      projects administered by others...☐
   c. Operational, i. e. engaged in designing and administering various kinds of research
      and other projects ....☐
   d. A combination of (a) and (b)..☐
   e. A combination of (a) and (c)..☐
   f. A combination of (b) and (c)..☐
   g. A combination of (a), (b), and (c)..☐
   h. Other (Please specify)_____☐

7. Chief executive officer:
   Name _____ Length of service as chief executive officer_____
   Title _____ Length of service in foundation _____

8. Total number of all *full-time* paid employees:_____ Number male_____ Number female_____

9. Total number of all *part-time* paid employees (excluding consultants) Number male____Number female____

10. Total number of all *paid* employees at executive level _____
    Full-time: Number male _____   Number female_____
    Part-time (excluding consultants) Number male_____ Number female_____

11. Total number of all employees at executive level who receive no compensation from any source:
    Number full-time_____Number part-time_____

12. Total number of *consultants* (excluding other part-time paid employees):
    Full-time: Number male_____   Number female_____
    Part-time: Number male_____   Number female_____

13. Typically, how many executive-level staff (paid or unpaid) are available for each of the following:

	Full-time	Part-time
Program activities		
Internal administrative duties (finance, etc.)................		
A combination of these duties..........................		

14. Did you hire your first executive-level staff member within the last four years? (Please check)
    On a full-time basis: ....Yes ☐.................................No ☐
    On a part-time basis: ....Yes ☐.................................No ☐

15. Do you contemplate hiring your first executive-level staff member within the next year? (Please check)
    On a full-time basis: .... Yes ☐.................................No ☐
    On a part-time basis: .... Yes ☐.................................No ☐

16. Please indicate highest academic degree for all full-time and part-time executive-level staff members,
    giving number of staff in each case:
    Ph.D. or equivalent ...._____ Bachelor's degree ......_____ Professional degree (law,
    Master's degree ...._____ No degree ...._____   medicine, etc.) ...._____

17. Please give the number of all full-time or part-time people on your executive-level staff who, prior to their
    employment by the foundation, have had experience in one or more of the following fields of employment:
    Another foundation ...._____   Full-time research ...._____
    Teaching............................_____   Medicine and public health ...._____
    Government service ...._____   Finance, business, and industry ...._____
    Administration of academic or other   Other (Please specify) ...._____
       non-profit organizations ...._____   _____

18. Has your foundation increased the number of its full-time or part-time staff over the last ten years? (Please check): . . . . Yes ☐ . . . . No ☐
If "yes," how many staff members have been added?. . . . . Full-time_____ Part-time_____
Please check reasons for expansion:
Growth in foundation's assets . . . . ☐   Other (Please specify) . . . . ☐
Growth in complexity of program . . . . ☐   _____
Need for greater degree of expertise . . . . ☐   _____

19. In which of the following ways are candidates for executive-level positions identified? Please rate *each item* from 0 to 5:
Recommendation by existing staff . . . . . . ._____   Candidate's participation in project
Informal recommendation by persons   financed by foundation . . . . ._____
  known to the staff ._____   Relationship or friendship with donor
Response to an application . . . . ._____   or donor's family . . . . ._____
Inquiry at universities . . . . ._____   Employment in donor's business . . . . ._____
Inquiry at executive placement centers . . ._____   Other (Please specify)_____

20. If appropriate to your situation, please indicate how many executive-level staff members were promoted to vacancies within the foundation, and how many staff members were brought in from outside the foundation in the last five years in lieu of promoting from within.
Promoted from within the foundation . . . ._____   Brought in from outside the foundation . . ._____

21. Do any full-time paid executive-level staff engage in some service outside the foundation for which they are compensated? (Please check) . . . . Yes ☐ . . . .No ☐

22. Is there a *mandatory* retirement age for executive-level staff? (Please check) . . . . .Yes ☐ . . . .No ☐
If "yes," please indicate age for: Males_____ . . . .Females_____
If "no," is there a *customary* retirement age for executive-level staff? (Please check) . .Yes ☐ . . . .No ☐
If "yes," please indicate age for: Males_____ . . . .Females_____

23. Please indicate the total number of executive-level staff who have left the foundation within the past four years: _____
Of those who did *not* leave for retirement, how many took jobs in each of the following:
Universities . . . . ._____   Non-profit organizations, institutes, etc.. . . ._____
Other foundations . . . . ._____   Finance, business, and industry . . . . ._____
Federal government. . . . . ._____   Other (Please specify)_____
State or local government . . . . ._____   _____

24. Please rate (from 0 to 5) in order of their importance *each* of the following qualifications for an effective foundation administrator:
Depth or extent of knowledge of   Ability to coordinate efforts of others . . . . ._____
  professional field ._____   Ability to maintain good relations with trus-
General knowledge . . . . ._____   tees and others outside the foundation. . ._____
Soundness of judgment . . . . ._____   Commitment to social improvement . . . . ._____
Administrative ability . . . . ._____   Imagination and creative capacity . . . . . . ._____
Ability to present ideas orally   Other (Please specify)_____
  and in writing . . . . ._____   _____

25. As a result of the recent legislation affecting foundations (Tax Reform Act of 1969), is it your opinion that in future recruiting, foundations will give more attention than formerly to one or more of the following? (Please check)   YES   NO
Specialized program expertise . . . . ☐ . . . . ☐ . . . .
Public relations and journalistic training . . . . ☐ . . . . ☐ . . . .
Industrial and accounting experience and training . . . . ☐ . . . . ☐ . . . .
Legal training . . . . ☐ . . . . ☐ . . . .
Will the legislation make the foundation field more or less attractive to potential staff members? (Please check) . . . . .More ☐ . . . . . Less ☐ . . . .

If "more," indicate why:_____

_____

_____

RANGE OF SALARIES, FEES, AND OTHER FORMS OF COMPENSATION

26. For each of the following positions please indicate below (a) compensation (exclusive of fringe benefits), (b) percent of professionally employed time which is devoted to foundation, (c) percent of total compensation for time devoted to foundation which is paid by foundation, and, if applicable, (d) other source of compensation for time devoted to foundation.

	Executive Head	Secretary	Treasurer	Assistant Secretary-Treasurer	Other (Title)
(a) Compensation for time devoted to foundation (exclusive of fringe benefits)					
(b) Percent of total professionally employed time which is devoted to foundation					
(c) Percent of total compensation paid by foundation for time devoted to foundation					
(d) Identify any other source of compensation for time devoted to foundation					

27. Does the foundation make a general practice of reviewing all executive-level salaries? (Please check)
Yes ☐ .... No ☐
If "yes," please indicate frequency of review and who makes it.
Annually ....☐   Chief executive ....☐
Biennially ....☐   Executive Committee....................☐
Other (Please specify) _____ _____☐   Personnel Committee ....☐
                                                     Other (Please specify)_____☐

28. Please check the fringe benefits listed below that are included in the executive-level staff's fringe benefit package, and indicate the year your foundation first instituted a pension plan.
Pension (Year instituted: Other medical and   Deferred compensation .....☐
    _____)...............☐   surgical insurance ....☐   Profit-sharing (company
Life insurance ....☐   Annual physical   foundations) ....☐
Major medical insurance ....☐   examinations............☐   Other (Please specify)_____
Blue Cross ....☐   Medical and hospital exami-
Blue Shield ....☐   nations after retirement ...☐   _____

29. Approximately what percent of the pension is paid for by the foundation, and what percent by the employee? ....By foundation _____% ....By employee _____%

30. Please check estimated "added on" value of foundation-financed fringe benefits to executive-level staff.
5-10% of salary ☐.......10-15% of salary ☐.......15-20% of salary ☐.......20-25% of salary ☐

31. What percent of highest salary does the foundation provide retiring executive-level staff under its retirement plan? ...._____%
Does the foundation rely entirely on the funded pension to achieve this percent? (Please check)
Yes ☐ No ☐ If "no," typically what percent is contributed by other than the funded source? _____%

32. What is the annual vacation period of executive-level staff? (Please check)
Two weeks □...........Three weeks □...........Four weeks □...........Over four weeks □
Does the foundation provide a sabbatical type of leave for executive-level staff? (Please check)
Yes □ No □ If "yes," how long? _____

33. Is it possible for an executive-level staff member to make grants or allocations within a trustee-approved program or in accordance with the terms of a trustee appropriation outside any specific program?
(Please check) ....Yes □ .... No □
If "yes," please indicate limitations on chart below by placing an X on the appropriate line.

	On his own authority	On his recommendation, with agreement from majority of staff	On his own, with ratification by head of foundation	Only by head of foundation	Other:
Such grants cannot exceed $5,000					
Such grants cannot exceed $10,000					
Such grants cannot exceed $25,000					
Such grants cannot exceed $50,000					
Other (Please specify)					

TRUSTEES OR DIRECTORS

34. How many trustees does the foundation have? ...._____

35. What is the average age of the existing board of trustees? (Please check)
Less than 50 years □.....50-55 years □.....55-60 years □.....60-65 years □.....65-70 years □

36. Do the trustees receive compensation? (Please check) ....Yes □ .... No □
If "yes," what is the range of payment? (Please check)
Over $50,000 □....$35,000-50,000 □....$20,000-35,000 □....$5,000-20,000 □....Under $5,000 □

37. How many members of the executive-level staff are members of the board?
Number: _____........................(If any, give title(s))_____

38. How frequently do the trustees meet? (Please check)
Less than once   Once a year ....□   Three times a year..□   More than quarterly □
a year ....□   Twice a year ......□   Quarterly ....□   On call ....□

39. How active a role do trustees have in the program of the foundation? (Please check as many as are appropriate.)
Determine foundation policy ....□   Discuss projects in detail at meetings ....□
Originate projects ....□   Ratify or deny projects at meetings ....□
Amend and develop projects ....□

40. What is the role of trustees in investment and other financial matters? (Please check)   YES   NO
Does the full board study and authorize investment changes? ....□ .... □
Is the board's nominal authority over investment matters
largely delegated to investment counsel? ....□ .... □
Is the board's nominal authority over investment matters
largely delegated to a bank or trust officer? ....□ .... □
Is there a special officer, who is in charge of invest-
ments, operating under the board? ....□ .... □

41. Does the foundation have a mixed trustee-staff committee for advisory and/or operational purposes? (Please check) ....Yes ☐ .... No ☐
If "yes," what is the role of the committee? (Please check)
To screen requests for grants ....☐   To review and evaluate projects ....☐
To make recommendations to the full board ....☐   Other (Please specify)_____☐

42. Does the foundation have special trustee committees for advisory and/or operational purposes? (Please check) ....Yes ☐ .... No ☐
If "yes," what are the roles of these committees? (Please check)
To screen requests for grants ....☐   To review and evaluate projects ....☐
To make recommendations to the full board ....☐   Other (Please specify)_____☐

43. Is there a *mandatory* retirement age for trustees? (Please check) ....Yes ☐ .... No ☐
If "yes," indicate age for: ....Males_____...............Females_____
If "no," is there a *customary* retirement age for trustees? (Please check) ....Yes ☐ .... No ☐
If "yes," indicate age for: ,,,,,, ...Males_____...............Females_____

44. Does the foundation have an *executive committee*? (Please check) ....   Yes ☐ .... No ☐
If "yes," does the committee include operating officers? ....Yes ☐ .... No ☐

45. How frequently does the executive committee meet? (Please check)
Once a year ....☐   Every other month ....☐
Twice a year ....☐   Once a month ....☐
Quarterly................................☐

46. What is the role of the executive committee? (Please check as many items as are relevant.)
A. To exercise the authority of the board:
by operating in lieu of board during periods between board meetings ....☐
by operating in lieu of board except for appointments and major grants ....☐
by authorizing grants and appropriations of a certain level (Please specify maximum level of
grant $_____, and of appropriation $_____) ....☐
by operating with board approval in principle to authorize grants and appropriations (Please
specify maximum level of grant $_____, of appropriation $_____)...☐
by recommending investments or determining financial policy ....☐
B. To screen agenda for trustees ....☐
C. To make preliminary appraisals of proposals to be submitted later to the board ....☐

The Study of the Foundation Administrator

Career Questionnaire
(For heads and staff members of foundations)

This is a confidential questionnaire; therefore you are free not to sign it or to use your name. If, however, you choose to sign it, the information you supply will not be identified with your name.

The questionnaire seeks information on *your* experience and personal opinions only, not your generalizations on the experiences and opinions of your colleagues. If a question has no application to your situation, please write "Not applicable" or "N.A." after the question.

SECTION 1

1. Descriptive rank or title:_____Age:_____Sex:_____

2. Please check highest degree: B.A. ☐ B.S. ☐ M.A. ☐ M.S. ☐ Ph.D. ☐ LL.B. ☐ J.D. ☐ D.Ed. ☐
   Other (please specify) _____
   Please check field in which degree was obtained:
   Social and behavioral sciences (including anthropology, education, psychology, history)........☐
   Physical and biological sciences (including mathematics) ....☐
   Humanities (including literature, philosophy, the fine and performing arts)....................☐
   Other (please specify)_____

3. Professional experience. (Please check any areas in which you have had experience prior to coming to the foundation.)
   Law ....☐   Business Administration (including
   Medicine (physician or surgeon) ....☐   accounting and banking) ....☐
   Health sciences (including dentistry, nursing,   Public Administration (any form of non-busi-
   & any para-medical profession or vocation).☐   ness or non-profit oriented administrative
   Teaching (at college or university level)......☐   experience, including academic adminis-
   Teaching (at other academic level)..........☐   tration—please specify which) _____☐
   Religion (religious education or religious   Engineering ....☐
   service) ....☐   Other (please specify)_____

4. How long with the foundation by which currently employed? _____Years

5. Please check whether present foundation employment is:.........full time ☐.........part time ☐

6. If part time, approximate percent of professionally employed time devoted to foundation: _____%
   If consultant, approximate percent of professionally employed time devoted to foundation: _____%

7. How did you come to the foundation's attention: (Please check)
   Through: Foundation's inquiries at executive
   Recommendation of member of   placement center ....☐
   foundation staff ....☐   Participation in project financed by foundation.☐
   Recommendation of third party known to staff.☐   Relationship or friendship with donor or
   Foundation's favorable response to a   donor's family ....☐
   personal application ....☐   Employment in donor's business ....☐
   Foundation's inquiries at universities ....☐   Other routes (please specify)_____☐

8. Earlier positions held in the foundation by which currently employed:

Position	Dates From:	To:
_____	_____	_____
_____	_____	_____
_____	_____	_____

9. Describe principal current responsibilities in foundation in three lines:

10. Last three positions held prior to employment by foundation: Dates

     Name of organization   Position   From: To:

11. What previous formal training or professional experience has in your opinion been especially helpful to you in your present foundation position? (Describe in three or four lines.)

12. Do you think that foundation administration could be improved if there were: Yes   No

formal university courses in foundation administration? .... ☐ .... ☐

internship programs within the foundation community? .... ☐ .... ☐

more information available in schools about foundations? .... ☐ .... ☐

If you would care to, please extend your comments on education and training for foundation service.

SECTION 2

13. How much interchange is there between you and the rest of the executive-level staff at your foundation, if there are other executives? (Please check)   Frequent   Occasional   Rare

On a formal basis .... ☐ .... ☐ .... ☐

On an informal basis .... ☐ .... ☐ .... ☐

14. How much contact is there between you and the following types of organizations? (Please check)   Frequent   Occasional   Rare

Other foundations .... ☐ .... ☐ .... ☐

Universities .... ☐ .... ☐ .... ☐

Government bureaus .... ☐ .... ☐ .... ☐

Research institutes .... ☐ .... ☐ .... ☐

Groups concerned with minority problems .... ☐ .... ☐ .... ☐

Other institutions—business or professional .... ☐ .... ☐ .... ☐

15. Please rate (from 0 to 5) *each* of the following qualifications in order of their importance for an effective foundation administrator: 5 INDICATES HIGHEST VALUE

Depth or extent of knowledge of professional field .... _____   Ability to present ideas orally and in writing .... _____

Commitment to social improvement .... _____   Ability to coordinate efforts of others .... _____

General knowledge .... _____   Ability to maintain good relations with trustees and with others outside the foundation... _____

Soundness of judgment .... _____

Administrative ability .... _____   Other (please specify)_____

16. Do you have an opportunity to influence decisions in the program, public information-personnel, and financial, operations of your foundation? (Please check as many as are appropriate.)

A. Program

By screening requests .... ☐

By examining projects in depth............ ☐

By participating in staff or other decision-making meetings .... ☐

By voting in staff meetings .... ☐

By making final decisions on grants .... ☐

By designing projects .... ☐

By directing or helping to operate projects ... ☐

By appearing before the trustees to discuss grants or projects .... ☐

By making formal recommendations on broad policy matters as well as on projects ...... ☐

B. Public Information-Personnel

By explaining foundation to the general public through formal or other reports ...... ☐

By lecturing on foundation's affairs .... ☐

By conducting seminars or the like on foundation matters .... ☐

By screening applicants for employment ...... ☐

By training new appointees .... ☐

C. Financial

By recommending investments .... ☐

By helping to determine financial policy ...... ☐

17. What are the major professional satisfactions of your job? (Please rate *each* of the following from 0 to 5.)

Association with others in foundation and in related professional fields .... _____
Investigating projects .... _____
Designing projects .... _____
Operating projects .... _____
Investigating programs .... _____

Evaluating projects or programs .... _____
Evaluating applications for grants .... _____
Engaging in academic research .... _____
Betting on good people .... _____
Seeing money used well .... _____
Other (please specify) _____

18. What are the major professional frustrations of your job? (Please rate *each* of the following from 0 to 5.)
5 INDICATES HIGHEST VALUE

Superficial investigation and appraisal of projects or programs .... _____
Lack of evaluation procedures for completed projects .... _____
Tendency of foundation to support special philanthropic interests of favored trustee or staff member .... _____
Pre-emption by trustees of the designing and investigative responsibility for most important projects .... _____
Nepotism .... _____
Failure of foundation to acknowledge merit or accomplishment and to promote from within ..... _____
Lack of encouragement of outside writing or research .... _____
Too little intellectual stimulation .... _____
Lack of time or opportunity to associate formally or informally with projects financed by the foundation .... _____
Lack of knowledge of, or experience with, projects financed by the foundation or problems to which foundation addresses itself .... _____
Lack of professional association with others in foundation field .... _____
Insufficient time to develop long-range projects .... _____
No opportunity to initiate and design projects .... _____
Inability to maintain place in professional field or discipline .... _____
Insufficient contact with superior or head of foundation .... _____
Difficulty in communicating ideas to trustees .... _____
Too much administrative paper work.. _____
Other (please specify) _____

19. What are the major economic frustrations of your job? (Please rate *each* of the following from 0 to 5.)

Unsatisfactory salary .... _____
No provision for salary review .... _____
No economic incentives .... _____

Unsatisfactory fringe benefits .... _____
Other (please specify) _____

20. How do you think foundation service could be made more attractive? (Please rate *each* of the following from 0 to 5.)

Greater involvement in designing and administering projects .... _____
Transforming grant-making foundations into operating foundations, at least in part .... _____
Greater job security, including tenure .... _____
Greater economic rewards .... _____
Special economic incentive for outstanding accomplishment .... _____
More generous and comprehensive fringe benefits .... _____
Loan of personnel to other foundations or organizations engaged in similar activities .... _____
Additional foundation-financed training for staff .... _____
Foundation encouragement of participation in professional meetings .... _____
Leave granted by foundation for special research or writing projects .... _____
Provision by foundation of something akin to a university sabbatical leave policy .... _____
Promotion from within .... _____

21. Please rate (from 0 to 5) *each* of the elements in the following list that in your opinion attract others to foundation service.

Opportunity to perform public service .... _____
Opportunity to aid underprivileged .... _____
Opportunity to foster research and intellectual development in the young .... _____
Opportunity to experiment with social reform .... _____
Opportunity to encourage growth in professional field or discipline .... _____

Professional association with like-minded individuals ....————
Opportunity to apply contemporary technology (such as the computer science) to education and
   research ....————
Financial rewards ....————
Travel ....————
Opportunity to influence given field of interest ....————
Opportunity to gain respected position in professional field or community ....————
Opportunity to gain wider public and professional recognition ....————

22. There are many ways of entering careers in the foundation field. Could you describe the events that led
to your first position? (In your answer, please indicate whether you planned or prepared for foundation
work.)

_____
_____
_____
_____

23. If you care to do so, we would welcome your comments on any aspects of your job that you feel have been
particularly rewarding in a professional sense

_____
_____
_____

**If you care to, please respond to any of the following questions that are applicable to your situation and
of interest to you.**

24. Do you feel that people outside your foundation understand the nature of your work? (Please check)
Yes ....☐   Most of the time ....☐   Rarely ....☐   No ....☐

25. If you stay in the foundation field, would you prefer to remain in your present foundation, or would you
like to move to another?
Prefer to remain in present foundation ......☐   Would like to move to another ....☐
Would like to leave foundation field for _____

26. Do you think your foundation is a better place to work than most others? (Please check)
Yes ....☐   No ....☐   Don't know ....☐

27. Do you think you have greater satisfactions in your job than most other people in the foundation field?
(Please check)
Yes ....☐   No ....☐   Don't know ....☐

28. Do you think that professional people outside the foundation world have greater satisfactions in their jobs
than you? (Please check)
Yes ....☐   No ....☐   Don't know ....☐

29. As a result of the recent legislation affecting foundations (Tax Reform Act of 1969), is it your opinion that
in future recruiting, foundations will give more attention than formerly to one or more of the following?
(Please check)
Specialized program expertise ....☐   Industrial and accounting experience & training .☐
Public relations and journalistic training .....☐   Legal training ....☐
Other (Please specify)_____

Will the legislation make the foundation field more or less attractive to potential staff members?
(Please check)   More ....☐   Less ....☐

Please give your reasons:_____
_____

Index